FROM ROCK BOTTOM

TO

ROCK STARS

WE SHINE MEDIA SOLUTIONS

Copyright © 2024 Dr. Tanya Davis

All rights reserved under International Copyright Law. Except as permitted under the U.S. Copyright Act of 1976, no part of this publication may be reproduced, distributed, or transmitted in any form or by any means, or stored in a database or retrieval system, without the prior written permission of the publisher.

Disclaimer ** The stories told are the individual author's version of life events as they took place. The author recognizes that other people's memories of the events described in the book may be different than their own. The details are not intended to hurt, defame, or offend anyone.

Publishing Company: WE Shine Media Solutions

Editing by: WE Shine Media Solutions

Front Cover: Vision N.O.W.

ISBN 978-1-304-54241-0

Visionary Author Dr. Tanya Davis

Co- Author Andrea Hancock et al. (2024)

Printed in: The United States, First Edition

FROM ROCK BOTTOM TO ROCK STARS

Dr. Tanya Davis, Visionary Author

Contributing Authors
CJ Colas
Dr. Kimberly Golden
Andrea Hancock
Duanechel Harris
Dr. Patricia Jackson
Christina Kelly
Minister Sylvia Page
Samahria Richie
Dr. Deidra Roussaw
Elbony Weatherspoon
Stephanie Whitlow-Wood
Chanta Wilder

TABLE OF CONTENTS

Chapter 1: I'm a Work of Art, a Masterpiece	6
About the Author – Dr. Tanya Davis	28
Chapter 2: Journey to a New Life	30
About the Author – CJ Colas	49
Chapter 3: The Not So Shrinking Violet	50
About the Author – Dr. Kimberly Golden	68
Chapter 4: A Journey of Becoming…	70
About the Author – Andrea Hancock	85
Chapter 5: Destination Success	87
About the Author – Duanechel Harris	104
Chapter 6: My Wings Are Finally Ready	106
About the Author – Dr. Patricia Jackson	115
Chapter 7: Believing in New Beginnings	116
About the Author – Christina Kelly	133

Chapter 8: Lady of Perfect Peace	134
About the Author – Minister Sylvia Page	146
Chapter 9: A Fork in the Road	148
About the Author – Samahria Richie	161
Chapter 10: The Journey to "I Do" (Love's Learning Curve)	163
About the Author – Dr. Deidra Roussaw	183
Chapter 11: It Was Perfect, Until It Wasn't	185
About the Author – Elbony Weatherspoon	206
Chapter 12: My Rise, My Fall, and My Redemption	208
About the Author – Stephanie Whitlow-Wood	226
Chapter 13: From Darkness to Light: A Journey of Resilience and Triumph	228
About the Author – Chanta Wilder	241

CHAPTER ONE
I'M A WORK OF ART, A MASTERPIECE
DR. TANYA DAVIS

DEDICATION

To God be the Glory!

This chapter delves into the incredible work of God. His blessings are not just showered upon us; He works through the hearts of His people to accomplish great things. Given its current state, the task I undertook in this chapter was particularly challenging. God sent angels to surround me in human form and inspired others to uplift me when I was pressing but sometimes struggling. I dedicate this chapter to my remarkable family and friends who provided affection, love, encouragement, and prayers day and night. Their support was pivotal to my success in achieving all my recent goals, and I am profoundly grateful.

Special thanks to my daughter Parisia Le`Marie Harp, who gave me a card that read:

Peace on Earth!

Momma, I know this has been a very challenging year, but you made it through. Your faith has and will continue to get you through. Always remember I am always rooting you on and always here.

I Love You!

To my Angels sent by God! Bestie Denise Turner, Sisters in Christ, Maryann Anello, Shawn Sims, Sonja Carney, and my therapist Pat Jackson. My friends and brothers in Christ, Gregory James, Kenneth Thirkield, Brother Al Winters, Bishop Chuck Middleton Jr. "It's coming together," Bishop Billy Walker "Walking in the Word," Chris Bond and Brandcocky Millionaire prayer call. To

Citipointe Church, Nashville Global Senior Pastors Mark & Leigh Ramsey, my Pastors Joel & Savannah Ramsey, Steve & Kathy Carter, and Greg & Mickey Taylor for leading the best Life Group ever! To Angela Lewis, you are a visionary and an outstanding publisher. Thank you.

To my grandchildren whom I adore, Tarien Marie Harp, Taylor A`Marie Harp, John "BJ" Foster, and one in particular, "King" Josiah Lee Foster, who gave me his unconditional love at my most vulnerable time in need.

Last but not least, a heartfelt tribute to my dear mother, Shirley Gene Harp, who may not be physically present but lives on vividly in my heart and soul. I will always hear your voice saying, "We fight; We never Quit." Rest in heaven, Momma!

For more information, visit:

www.WomenwhorockNashville.org

www.Fromcracktochrist.net

Tanya@livingtn.com

Cell: 615.926.9935 Office: 888.519.5113 ext. 343

I'M A WORK OF ART, A MASTERPIECE
DR. TANYA DAVIS

A masterpiece is a creation of exceptional artistry, skill, or craftsmanship that stands as the epitome of a particular artist's or creator's work. This term is commonly used to characterize works that exhibit outstanding quality, innovation, and a profound impact within their respective fields. Masterpieces manifest in various forms of artistic expression, such as painting, sculpture, literature, music, film, and other creative pursuits. The designation implies a level of mastery and excellence, elevating the work to a pinnacle of achievement within its context.

In this chapter, we encounter a woman whose divinely orchestrated life journey has propelled her from the depths of adversity to a transformative state designed by God—molding, shaping, and reinventing her in a unique manner. She emerges not as an ordinary creation of the world's choices but as a masterpiece in the eyes of God.

Dr. Tanya Davis, once known by aliases like "Tanya Harp," "Terrible T," and "T Baby" in Detroit, Michigan, famously referred to as "Motown" due to the influence of Berry Gordy—a man of vision, drive, talent, and determination. Detroit, renowned for its exceptional vehicles and serving as the epicenter of the automobile industry, boasts that one in every six working Americans was directly or indirectly associated with the auto industry, with Detroit housing the "Big Three" auto firms—General Motors, Ford Motor Company, and Chrysler.

Growing up in this vibrant city led to inspiration-fueled dreams of driving beautiful cars and achieving fame by making it to the top. Here, I recount my journey through time and my own obsession with riding in coveted vehicles such as the 1975 Ford Elite, the 1977 Firebird Sky Bird by Pontiac, the 1979 Corvette, the 1981 Datsun 280ZX, the 1988 Cadillac Cimarron, the 1990 convertible Mustang, the Ford of Europe Merkur XR4Ti, the 1995 BMW, 1998 Mercedes 190E, 2000 Saab, 2003 Audi A4 convertible, the 2006 Jaguar, the BMW LI, the 2017 Mustang convertible, 2018 Jeep Cherokee, and presently the Mercedes 450 convertible—creating a remarkable timeline of experiences that elicit a heartfelt "WOW!"

I grew up as an only child spoiled by my grandparents, my parents, and other close friends of my parents claiming to be Godparents, yearning for acceptance from everyone around me. To fill the void, I bestowed family titles upon those I encountered—brother, sister, cousin, auntie, uncle. In my preliminary stages, even the parents of the person with whom I shared my first intimate moment became "mom and dad" in my address book. My aspirations were inspired by their lifestyle of a pristine home, luxury cars, a boat, and a ranch with horses. As time passed, my desires evolved from material possessions to include a penchant for name-brand clothes, shoes, handbags, and an affinity for ostentatious jewelry—a walking homage to Mr. T, and the allure of furs added a touch of extravagance to my lifestyle.

However, this pursuit led me down a destructive path. In my inaugural novel, "From Crack to Christ," I laid bare the tumultuous journey, chronicling the highs and lows. Even after celebrating 33 years of sobriety, the challenges persisted. Life, relationships, managing a business, assuming leadership roles, overseeing a salon, orchestrating events—the hurdles are unceasing. The memory of enduring the cast's frustration and demands for money while struggling to meet payroll for stage plays lingers. Despite knowing it wasn't a failure on my part, it became a life of darkness.

In those darker moments, when contemplation of escape and surrender loomed large, it was divine intervention that transformed my mindset. God began to provide me with the strength to persevere, encouraging me to stand tall, relying solely on His guidance. As I walked hand in hand with the divine, occasional whispers of despair surfaced but gradually waned.

Throughout the years, I found myself navigating the path of entrepreneurship, not out of choice, but due to a lingering felony that cast a shadow over my professional life. The struggle to secure traditional employment was vividly etched in my memory. I recall the night I slept outside, determined to secure a job at General Motors. Miraculously, I obtained two applications, completing both—one for myself and the other for my daughter's father. Despite putting in all the effort, it was he who secured the position and eventually retired from that very job.

The pursuit continued with an attempt to join Northwest Airlines. I completed the requisite ninety days, demonstrating punctuality and earning praise as one of the top performers in my department. However, my honesty in leaving the question about past criminal history unanswered on my application came back to haunt me during a second review. Though they acknowledged my contributions, they were compelled to let me go due to oversight. While I could have faced legal consequences for potential fraud, they chose not to press charges.

This experience left an indelible mark on my approach to job applications. The stigma of being labeled a felon made the application process a constant uphill battle despite my efforts to seek out opportunities deemed "felon-friendly." The journey, shaped by resilience and tenacity, led me down the path of entrepreneurship as I worked to overcome the barriers imposed by a single, haunting incident.

I emerged from the crucible of adversity as a successful cosmetologist owning three thriving salons spanning from Detroit to Nashville. It was in the lion's den, an unexpected place of discovery, that I unearthed a latent talent bestowed upon me by God. The constraints of that challenging environment led me to cut my own hair using a toenail clipper, as traditional scissors were deemed contraband. The unseen benefit was the ample practice I gained by cutting and styling the hair of fellow inmates.

Upon my release, a pair of scissors placed in my hands transformed me into a modern-day Edward Scissorhands. With an innate ability to visualize and execute, I became proficient in precision cuts, razor cuts, disconnected cuts—you name it, I could effortlessly bring it to life. This divine gift, honed in the most unlikely setting, propelled me into a successful career where I sculpted not only human hair but also tackled the intricacies of bushes, dogs, and more. The journey from confinement to mastery became a testament to the transformative power of resilience and the unexpected talents that can emerge from the most challenging circumstances and become a Masterpiece.

I didn't anticipate this evolving into a career, but it was intricately designed, an integral part of God's plan for my life. Reflecting on…

1 Thessalonians 5:18, "In everything give thanks; for this is God's will for you in Christ Jesus," and…

James 4:15, "Instead, you ought to say, 'If the Lord wills, we will live and also do this or that," I recognized the divine orchestration at play…

Psalm 143:10 further guided me: *"Teach me to do Your will, For You are my God; Let Your good Spirit lead me on level ground."*

Many grappled with the quest to discern God's will for my life, questioning purpose and divine plans. Yet, His will transcends earthly objectives. It's about shaping us into holy beings who find profound joy and freedom amidst the challenges of a fallen world.

Witnessing God's transformative work in my life, my faith grew, especially when I realized that aligning with His will was the most pleasing thing to Him. Trusting His words became paramount, and I began to not only hear sermons but actively engage with His teachings. Applying these principles in real-life situations and responding to every scripture as it became relevant marked a transformative journey. It wasn't about just attending services on Sundays or Bible studies; it was about living out the lessons and trusting in His guidance through every circumstance.

I can't share with others that "weeping may endure for a night and joy comes in the morning" without it being a profound truth etched into the fabric of my own life. Telling others to "lean not on your own understanding" while struggling with my own understanding was a stark reality I wanted to confront on my journey as a Christian and a woman of God. This path wasn't easy; I traversed through devastating situations that demanded a true commitment to being a doer of His Word. In the crucible of trial and error, I began to understand God's process in creating a work of art—myself.

The journey persisted with daily tests, constant trials, and enduring sufferings, but the transformative benefits became increasingly evident. Through these challenges, I witnessed the growth and strength that only comes from following Jesus. In embracing His light and example, I discovered a wellspring of joy, happiness, and peace, even amidst the hardships.

The importance of following Jesus lies in the profound transformation that occurs. As Matthew 19:28-29 NLT aptly states, "*Everyone who has given up houses or brothers or sisters or father or mother or children or property, for My sake, will receive a hundred times as much in return and will inherit eternal life.*"

God provided this verse to help me understand that my loss and losing tangible things also have benefits. While the specific nature of this reward is not detailed, its superiority over any earthly reward is unquestionable. It's a call to surrender and trust, knowing that the journey, though challenging, leads to unparalleled and eternal fulfillment in Christ. You reach new dimensions. People around you will begin to understand something clearly in you without question and share how they've seen a change. The things you have gone through will help others in their endeavors.

In 2020, a year I was navigating well, the world was abruptly reminded of its shortcomings as the pandemic swept through, defying wealth or privilege. It was a stark revelation that we were all vulnerable regardless of financial status. As the U.S. Department of Homeland Security defined essential workers—those who risked their lives to sustain critical infrastructure—our lives were altered. We lost loved ones, and even as we emerged from the pandemic, the world felt irrevocably changed.

Moving forward, a collective realization dawned: we all needed mental health support, which was once considered taboo. The pandemic exposed our vulnerabilities, affecting not just our physical health but also our emotional well-being. I personally experienced this in the loss of my mother on May 20, 2020—a pivotal figure, my confidante, and the one I turned to in times of need and for prayer. Her absence left a void, pushing me to seek solace in God's voice and prompting me to truly listen and reflect.

Amidst the solitude, my marriage faced challenges. Though physically separated due to our living arrangements, the emotional distance became apparent. Despite attempts to rekindle the flame, it was evident that we were merely coexisting and not fulfilling each other's needs. The pandemic underscored the importance of seizing opportunities, prompting me to reassess the relationship. In acknowledging our growing apart, I summoned the courage to make a decision that would liberate both of us—pursuing happiness, finding compatibility, and making a conscious choice to live under one roof and be united in purpose. It wasn't an easy choice, but it was necessary for our individual growth and well-being.

Every day, I express gratitude to God that both of us understood the assignment and have managed to remain friends even today. I've always wished the best for him, and he reciprocates the sentiment. It's been two years since our separation, and I'm genuinely thrilled that he has found happiness in a new marriage.

For me, this period served as an opportunity for self-improvement, a chance to prepare myself to be a great wife—not perfect, but great. In pursuit of this goal, I accomplished significant milestones. I became a licensed minister of the Gospel, earned an honorary doctorate in Leadership, received another honorary doctorate in Christian Humane Letters, and pursued education to become a licensed Realtor. However, despite these achievements, the journey took its toll in unexpected ways...

On December 20, 2022, I embarked on a significant chapter in my life by deciding to sell my home. Unemployment since 2020 compelled me to focus on organizing our annual gala, channeling some of its proceeds to support various 501c3 organizations. However, a shift in the Board of Directors' priorities redirected efforts toward establishing transitional housing for women—a long-held dream of mine. Faced with financial distress, I rationalized that selling my home, extracting equity, and starting anew was a logical step.

Seeking divine guidance, I prayed, and a clear message resonated: "Everything New." This guided me to a new church, Citipointe Nashville, where I found warmth and welcome in this vibrant community. Their friendliness, coupled with a newfound church family, set the stage for a transformative journey.

At Citipointe, during a profound sermon about love and faith in action, the book of James espouses more than any other book in the New Testament. James places the spotlight on the necessity for believers to act in accordance with their faith. In verse nine, James wrote that those who truly trust our Lord and Savior can boast about their exalted position, even if they're completely destitute in this life. The lowliest Christian believer is eternal royalty with endless riches through their faith in Jesus. We should call our worst moments joyful because trials help us trust God more.

In a moment of vulnerability, when Pastor asked if anyone needed prayer, I stood before the congregation, sharing my journey of celebrating thirty-two years of sobriety and the challenging decision to sell my home because interest rates had risen. The response was immediate and miraculous, as realtors from the congregation offered assistance.

As my home hit the market, I juggled real estate school while navigating the complexities of the selling process. Remarkably, within a week, I had a contract placed on my home. The deal progressed smoothly until a potential setback emerged—the underwriter discovered a restitution claim that threatened to absorb the proceeds.

Battling disappointment, I faced the reality that a massive portion of ninety percent of my hard-earned investment would be lost. However, the message of "Everything New" resonated louder than the challenges. Deciding to move forward, I embraced a season of new beginnings, acknowledging that any equity in my home would always be claimed by my restitution.

My journey continued, propelled by faith and determination. Engaged in real estate school, I prepared for the 2023 annual award gala, embodying the spirit of moving forward despite the hurdles. Each step reaffirmed the transformative power of faith, community, and the resilience to embrace a new chapter in life. However, it serves as a constant reminder that when God imparts a vision, instructions, goals, and dreams, it doesn't guarantee a journey free from trials and tribulations. Indeed, this road gets deeper…

Bottom of Form

I found myself in need of a job. During the COVID-19 pandemic, my shoulder became frozen due to years of blow-drying, exacerbated by a year of inactivity due to the lockdown. Upon resuming, carpal tunnel syndrome in my hands became evident, causing my fingers to involuntarily clench. Standing for extended periods resulted in back pain, and a visit to the chiropractor revealed the sorry state of my spine. Doctors advised therapy, but lacking proper insurance coverage made it an expensive option. In light of this, I decided to explore job opportunities.

The job search presented unexpected hurdles. The past issues on my record, which I thought were resolved, resurfaced during background checks, necessitating their removal. Despite my extensive customer service experience and caregiving background, one prospective employer adhered to a policy that excluded individuals with certain criminal histories—it was a disheartening setback.

Receiving support from friends and selling items from my home and valuable jewelry sustained me. Though income from a few clients and occasional book sales provided some relief, it was inconsistent. This was a challenging time.

Amidst this, I faced the daunting task of organizing "Women Who Rock Nashville," an event I contemplated canceling. However, the prayers, encouragement, and unwavering support from my loved ones, coupled with the belief that I can do all things through Christ, who strengthens me, propelled me forward. Sensing the event's potential impact, Satan sought to intervene, attempting to thwart the completion of the third year of our successful event and the potential sponsorship dollars that could follow. The struggle intensified, but my reliance on faith became crucial in overcoming these obstacles and reaching the event's full potential. But God! Again, a sold-out successful gala.

I then successfully completed the A and B portions of my real estate studies; however, after the intensive work on the "Women Who Rock Nashville" event, I realized I needed to revisit the material for the exam. Even though I had already completed the course, I chose to do a retake as a viewer to reinforce my knowledge. After dedicating four weeks to intensive study, I felt confident enough to take the state and national exams.

I passed the exam; however, the subsequent steps involved getting fingerprinted and filling out the application, which included questions about my past. Disclosing my felon status prompted a process of researching documents, obtaining release from parole, and writing letters to the judge to release necessary paperwork. Though proven untrue, a challenging incident in Nashville added another layer of complexity.

Managing these matters during a tumultuous period made me question my decisions, but an unwavering trust and belief in a brighter future kept me going. I immersed myself in faith, attending Bible studies, prayer calls, and life group sessions, ensuring the Word was ever-present. While bills piled up and the fridge stayed empty, I maintained my sanity by attending events, giving back to the community, and speaking at graduations.

I had faced financial uncertainty, ran an organization, and planned an award gala, but there was still nothing for myself. However, unexpected blessings poured in—cash apps from family and friends, even strangers, and calls from organizations wanting to honor me. Grateful for every bit of support, I found strength in knowing that God had me all the time. In the midst of adversity, my sister in Christ kept me looking regal, and God's grace made sure I appeared as a queen of excellence—joyful, with an unrivaled smile that no challenge could erase.

Despite the relentless presence of a figure named Satan, I persevered in resisting his ceaseless attempts to fulfill his sinister agenda of killing, stealing, and destroying me on a daily basis. Armed with the word of God, I engaged in a constant battle using the scriptures as my powerful weapon, holding onto trust and unwavering belief. Each day, as I woke up with a smile, Satan would insidiously remind me of all my troubles, whispering dark suggestions such as ending my own life by jumping off the balcony or consuming the entire bottle of medicine. In those moments, I had to assert my identity and rebuff his malevolent influence. I would firmly declare that I am a child of the King, the Almighty, and command him to leave my mind. I reminded him that his opportunity to destroy me had passed, and his power over me was canceled.

In defiance, I would raise my voice, vehemently expressing my disdain for Satan from the depths of my heart. I made it clear that I disliked him just as much as he despised me. Our mutual aversion was unmistakable, and I declared, "You had your chance, and if you couldn't succeed then, you certainly can't now! I hate you. Our feelings are mutual – you don't like me, and I don't like you. Let's be clear about that!"

This would happen periodically, but my relationship with my Father, my Daddy, my God grew tremendously. Satan will try to get you in a space or season where it feels like you've done something wrong, so you start repenting for things you've done, hoping that God is not punishing you for something in your past…Remember This!

"No one, I repeat, No One, is currently being punished by God for any sin, no matter how grievous. On the contrary, we're all being called into repentance and believe in the one He sent, Jesus Christ, who bore our sins and was crushed on the cross for our offenses and, moreover, was raised from the dead for our justification. It would be beyond senseless for Him to punish anyone for the sins He already forgave!" ~~ *Lehlohonolo Gordons*

In a season like this, it's crucial to recognize that there are valuable lessons to learn. God was preparing me for the next level of my journey. During such times, your focus will shift—seek Him more, listen more intently, pray more fervently, and experience personal growth. As I navigated this period, I noticed that people, places, and things naturally shed themselves from my shoulders, and I didn't even notice, all the while making my burdens lighter. Even though I may feel like I was in a lonely place, I had to remember that I'm never alone—God had me exactly where He wanted me. My worship became more profound, becoming a refuge in times of trouble.

Expectations arose for things to turn around, but the anticipated changes seem delayed. I found myself questioning the Lord, feeling dissatisfied and disappointed despite my trust and belief. However, at a pivotal moment, I realized that I still trust Him, my belief remains unshaken, and I feel good. I ask myself why I persist when things aren't changing. I've reached a point where there's no one else to lean on; I placed it all in His hands…

Still facing financial challenges with zero income, I humbly accepted support from loved ones because I recognized that God uses people to get the job done. Your daughter, in a commendable act of kindness, pays your rent. While grateful for her assistance, you cry out to God, recognizing the need for a faster resolution… "Lord, she can't take care of me and four kids." Your brother loans you money, and you borrow it against your life insurance policy to pay him back because he needs his money. I had to humble myself as contributions from my ex-husband, best friend, ex-boyfriend, sisters in Christ, and others poured in, creating a complex tapestry of assistance during an admittedly embarrassing moment in my life.

Simultaneously, I passionately continue to pursue my career in real estate, leveraging various free trials for products and free trials employing marketing strategies, including creating branding materials and videos with an old photoshoot because I couldn't afford to get a new one. Despite the financial struggles, my trust and belief in God became a well-practiced science. This focus kept me moving forward, and remarkably, no one around me truly knew the extent of my challenges because I refused to let anything steal my joy. They still saw me smiling, with joy in my heart because I was moving in the anointing. The power of the relationship I've cultivated with God becomes evident—although lacking in financial resources, my joy is abundant. Going to sleep and waking up with a smile, I encourage myself and inspire others along the way. It was such a beautiful gift to see the demonstration of God's love and His grace fall upon me…This made it easy to continue to trust Him!

The LORD says: *"Cursed is the one who trusts in man, who depends on flesh for his strength and whose heart turns away from the LORD. He will be like a bush in the wastelands; he will not see prosperity when it comes. He will dwell in the parched places of the desert, in a salt land where no one lives."*

I began to catch a glimpse of sunlight after seven weeks of becoming a real estate agent when a friend referred me to my first client from Jackson, TN. Commuting two hours daily for two years, she sought to relocate, especially with her daughter entering college in Nashville. I found a home in Burns, TN, just 22 minutes from her job, 15 minutes from college, and 5 minutes off the freeway. Securing a contract and finding a home they both loved brought me joy, but challenges lingered.

Navigating through the holiday season was rough. We initiated an appraisal, but with limited business days, I had to request an addendum for a new closing date, shifting from December 22 to December 29. The anticipation of closing right before the new year, receiving a commission, and starting to repay people filled me with excitement, but alas, that day did not materialize as expected. What do you do when disappointment continues to surface?

Hebrews 10:35-36: *"Do not throw away your confidence, which has a great reward."* When disappointment strikes, hold tightly to your faith. Say, "I am still confident. I still believe."

Maintaining this type of confidence in God and in yourself will require mental and spiritual effort, but it is your road to better things. All I could do was repeatedly affirm, "I'm still confident this deal will happen. Lord, I still believe this deal will close." These became my two new mantras, anchoring me in focus, unwavering faith, and stability. Entrusting it to God, I headed to Clarksville to spend the holidays with my daughter and grandchildren.

During the drive, those familiar doubts tried to creep in, whispering that I had nothing to give and was financially strained. Yet, in that moment, I reminded myself of the invaluable gifts God was bestowing upon me—His love and grace. Embracing this realization, I offered my loved ones the most precious gift I had—myself.

As Christmas arrived, I awakened with the understanding that the true celebration was not about gifts but the birth of Jesus Christ. It transcends a Christian holiday or festival, going beyond the mere decoration of houses. It's an opportunity to pause and express gratitude for the love, hope, and joy found in Jesus—our Savior, Father, and Friend. This perspective transformed Christmas into a meaningful celebration of divine love and grace.

We gathered together to prepare our Christmas dinner, indulging in the joy of cooking, playing games, and watching heartwarming Christmas movies. In the midst of this festive atmosphere, my daughter handed me a card containing a thoughtful monetary gift. Additionally, my youngest granddaughter surprised me with two exquisite bottles of perfume, each fragrance capturing my heart and evoking tears of joy. Their gestures of love and understanding, acknowledging my situation, made the holiday even more special.

Despite ongoing tribulations, I consciously chose to relegate them to the background while maintaining trust and belief. It is possible to navigate through life without succumbing to fear, worry, and stress. I've discovered the power of relying on faith. Reflecting on my journey, I realize that every step I've taken has been rooted in faith.

Credit for this perspective goes to Pastor Charles Middleton of Mt. Zion Missionary Baptist Church in Detroit. He immersed the entire congregation in Hebrews 11:1, emphasizing that *"faith is confidence in what we hope for and assurance about what we do not see."* Although I didn't fully grasp the significance at the time, the lasting impact of that teaching has become clear to me now.

Understanding the essence of faith brings to mind a crucial aspect of pleasing God and how important it is. Hebrews 11:6 underscores this, stating, *"But without faith, it is impossible to please Him, for he who comes to God must believe that He is and that He is a rewarder of those who diligently seek Him."* This recognition reinforces the notion that faith is not just a passive concept but an active pursuit that aligns us with the divine, and it opens the door to God's rewarding grace for those earnestly seeking Him…That's why it's so important!

I often hear others say, "Girl, I'd still be crying over the losses from the sale of your home." But why? There's nothing I can do to change it. I could cry for days, but what would it achieve? Absolutely nothing. Focusing on the past only keeps you bound. It's crucial to understand that life is filled with challenges, and how you navigate them determines your destination. When God designs your life, it's a work of art in progress, a masterpiece in the making. As Jeremiah tells us, He already knows the plans He has for us, but sometimes we deviate from that path, and He knows that, too.

Life is much like an artist's canvas. Paint various pictures, and you'll have more than one. The key is to learn from your mistakes, trials, and tribulations. God is molding you, creating a unique masterpiece. Once you grasp this, you can endure the punches life throws because you know that at the end of the season, you WIN. He had you all along.

Enjoy life; don't let it shake you. I've experienced significant growth through lessons with family, friends, organizations, and church. One must man their post, regardless of life's challenges. Utilize knowledge and wisdom, and remember, we don't fight in the physical realm; we let God oversee our battles. He encourages us to rest, take a nap, or even watch a good movie, and you can accomplish this when you genuinely believe in Him and His word. Faith is action, as James 1:22 reminds us, *"But be doers of the word, and not hearers only, deceiving yourselves."* I strive daily to be a doer of the word, applying its principles to my life and embracing all the vibrant colors of life.

Distance yourself from negativity entering your ear gates. There may be moments when you need to disconnect, turn off your phone, and spend time on self-reflection while holding onto your beliefs. I believe the transaction with my client's home will close. As the saying goes, "He may not come when you want him, but he's always right on time."

Thank you, Lord, for hearing my prayers, for your faithfulness, and for the warrior spirit you have placed in me; thank you for showering me with vision, talent, and grace. I will continue my attitude of gratitude. Thank you, Lord. My future is safe, and all my promises are secure in you!

Genesis 21:22, *"And it came to pass at that time that Abimelech and Phichol, the chief captain of his host, spake unto Abraham, saying, God is with thee in all that thou doest."*

These past twelve months presented numerous challenges, but I've overcome them all. I illuminated the night with my smile, radiating a brightness that concealed the struggles within. It wasn't about hiding; instead, it was a testament to standing tall and displaying what I've learned from God. I'm not afraid to share my picture with the world because I've embraced transparency. Every facet of me is a vision akin to a portrait of the Mona Lisa. Now, those tribulations appear as vibrant colors on my canvas. "Recognizing that I am a work of Art, and God is creating a Masterpiece."

ABOUT THE AUTHOR - DR. TANYA DAVIS

Dr. Tanya Davis is a dynamic entrepreneur, author, inspirational speaker, producer, professional beauty educator, mentor, and playwright. As a witness to the transformative power of love and redemption, she actively serves as a licensed minister of the Gospel, engaging in impactful ministry work. Through her compelling testimony, lives have been saved, and she has inspired countless individuals to overcome obstacles. Driven by a passion for spreading hope, she particularly focuses on guiding those grappling with addiction, domestic violence, and mental health issues toward successful recovery.

A dedicated philanthropist, Dr. Davis generously volunteers her time for various organizations, including Operation Stand-down Tennessee, Mending Hearts, The Next Door, G4 facility Level 3 Residential Treatment, Tennessee Women Prison, Salvation Army, Women with Open Arms, Nashville Recovery Fest, and others. Additionally, she motivates students by participating in career days at elementary schools, high schools, and cosmetology schools, imparting wisdom about perseverance and the importance of rejecting drugs. Her vision for the future remains guided by her unwavering faith, stating, "Wherever GOD leads me because I know it is HIS purpose!"

Dr. Davis boasts an impressive array of achievements, including the Phenomenal Woman Distinguished Award, Spirit of Excellence Award, and the I Am Royalty Award. She proudly serves as a National Spokeswoman for Beauty Behind Bars, traveling nationally and internationally. Recent accolades include the "Partnership Award" from

Pass the Beauty Organization, the "IAAWE Leadership Award" in Atlanta, GA, Unstoppable Women in Business, Uterine Cancer Foundation "Superhero Award," Rock the Bell Foundation "Girl, You So Dope Award," the Varnell Foundation Legacy Award and Nashville Business Journal "Women of Influence." She holds an Honorary Doctorate in Leadership from the MIZ CEO Society International Coaching Institute and a Doctorate of Christian Humane Letters from the School of the Great Commission Theological Seminary.

Dr. Davis is a devoted mother to her daughter Parisia Harp and a proud grandmother of four precious grandchildren: Tarien Harp, Taylor Harp, John "BJ" Foster, and Josiah "JoJo" Foster. She holds dear the unwavering support of her number one fan and ride-or-die, her mother, Shirley Gene Harp, who prayed for her restoration from the depths of despair and encouraged her to fulfill God's plan for her life. Although her mother passed away on May 20, 2020, her spirit continues to live on in Dr. Davis's heart.

Finally, Dr. Davis firmly believes in the power of encouraging change, recognizing its necessity, and relying on the strength of her faith in Christ.

CHAPTER TWO
JOURNEY TO A NEW LIFE
CJ COLAS

DEDICATION

I would like to thank the Almighty God for this opportunity to live and write my story.

This book is dedicated to my wonderful family: my wonderful parents, my wonderful husband Steeve, my beautiful son SJ, my daughter Jasmine, my siblings Rik, Tosha, Jr., and Archie, and friends who are family, like Mirleine, Daphne, Yolanda, Sherrie, and many others… I can't name them all because it would be another book. I love you all.

JOURNEY TO A NEW LIFE

CJ COLAS

The Reflection

"How did I get here? What have I done in my life that caused me to get here?" I have asked myself these questions many times, and wished I could go back and change so many things. But I have learned that it wasn't what I have done; it was life. I'll give you a quick version of how I got to where I am today.

Throughout our lives, we make countless choices that shape our experiences and ultimately lead us to where we are today. Reflecting on these choices can be a valuable exercise in self-awareness and personal growth. In this book, I will explore the factors that have contributed to the person I have become and the role that my actions and decisions have played in my life's journey.

From the very beginning of life, we are presented with a series of choices that set the stage for our future. These choices can be as simple as what we wear or what we eat, to more significant decisions like where we go to school or what career path we choose. As we get older, we are constantly faced with new choices and challenges that can have lasting impacts on our lives.

To understand how I got to where I am today, I must examine the choices and experiences that have shaped my life. This may involve looking back at key moments, such as my upbringing, education, and relationships. By examining these experiences and the choices I made at each stage, I can gain a deeper understanding of the factors that have contributed to my current circumstances.

One of the most significant factors in determining where I am today is the choices I have made in my career. My career is often a reflection of my interests, values, and goals. By evaluating my chosen career path and the decisions that led me there, I can gain insight into how my professional experiences have influenced my life.

Another important aspect to consider is the relationships I've formed throughout my life. The people we surround ourselves with can have a significant impact on our personal growth and development. By reflecting on the relationships I have cultivated, I can better understand how they have shaped my life and contributed to my current situation.

In addition to examining your personal journey, it is crucial to recognize that life itself is a significant factor in determining where you are today. Life is full of surprises and unpredictable events that can change the course of your life in an instant. It is essential to acknowledge that sometimes, life events are beyond our control, and we must learn to adapt and grow from these experiences.

The Beginning

Growing up in Miami, Florida, with my parents, siblings, and friends was a defining period of my life. I cherish the memories of my wonderful childhood, which shaped me into the person I am today. Coming from a Haitian household, I am grateful for the unique upbringing that instilled invaluable life lessons and cultural richness in me. The fusion of American upbringing with Haitian heritage has not only brought humor into my life but also imparted essential values that guide me through each day. The

Haitian way of nurturing children and instilling distinct values remains a cornerstone of my identity, transcending the influence of American culture. As I journey through adulthood, I carry with me the profound gratitude and pride of being a Haitian woman, which I plan to pass on to my children.

High school and college are often regarded as the best years of a person's life. This is a time when we as kids are given more freedom and independence, while still being surrounded by a supportive community or family. During these years, I built lifelong friendships, pursued new experiences, and laid the foundation for my future career.

My name is CJ Colas, and I moved to Nashville, TN, from Miami, FL, a few years ago with my husband. We have been together since high school, and if I had to go back and choose, I would pick him a thousand times again. We have two beautiful children, and I am grateful for the family we have created. I learned in this life that the person you choose to make a life with is extremely important. You never know how your life can change in an instant.

In April 2016, I started bleeding from what I thought was a heavy menstrual cycle. After bleeding for about 12 days, I scheduled an appointment to see my gynecologist to determine why I was bleeding so much and why it didn't seem like it was stopping anytime soon.

During my appointment, the doctor performed an ultrasound, took my vitals, and informed me that the bleeding was due to fibroid tumors and would eventually stop. He recommended that I take birth control to regulate my cycle. I took birth control for an entire month, but the bleeding did not stop; in fact, it became worse. I returned to the doctor and explained what was happening, but he simply prescribed more birth control. I continued to see the doctor month after month, but he was unable to help me.

By August 2016, I was feeling weak and tired. The bleeding was becoming more frequent and severe, and I didn't know what to do. One day at work, I had a heavy bleeding accident that soaked my clothes. This had never happened before. I removed my blazer and tied it around my waist before leaving work early and calling the doctor. At the time, I lived about 10-15 minutes from work. When I got home, the bleeding was worse than ever, and my car was a mess. I went into the shower to clean up and had blood clots falling out of me like rain. I was scared and stayed in the shower until the water started getting cold. I called the doctor's office and let them know what was happening. The doctor asked me to go to the emergency room the next morning and said he would meet me there. He wanted to perform a DNC, or dilation and curettage, to scrape out the blood clots and stop the bleeding.

Early Tuesday morning, my husband and I prayed as we do every morning. We then took our son to daycare and drove to the emergency room. I was nervous about the procedure, but the doctor assured me that it was an outpatient procedure and would be successful. I still felt scared, so I prayed to God for healing and protection.

When we arrived at the hospital, they took my vitals, drew blood, and told me to wait in one of the ER rooms. The nurse returned and said they needed to do the blood test again. I was curious as to why they needed more blood, but shortly after, my doctor came into the room and told my husband and I that the first lab results showed that I was pregnant. He knew I wasn't pregnant, so he wanted to do more tests.

I was relieved at first, thinking that I had been pregnant the entire time and had just miscarried. However, I was also sad because I had wanted another child. My husband assured me that everything would be all right, but I was upset with my doctor for missing the pregnancy for months.

The doctor came back into the room and apologized for missing "something." He said that he didn't see a fetus and wasn't sure where it could be. He thought that it might be in my tubes, but the blood test results indicated that I should have been at least nine months pregnant. He admitted me to the hospital so that they could run more tests and do a body scan to find the fetus. I assumed that the fetus had fallen out when I was clotting in the bathroom the day before, but I wanted them to tell me for sure. I am not an expert, and one thing I have learned is not to assume anything. I have also learned that some doctors may do the same based on what they are told.

By the afternoon, I was assigned to a regular room in the hospital. I told my husband to go home and pick up our son from daycare. He left at around 4:30 pm. I had a CT scan that evening and waited for the test results. My husband called me afterward, and we stayed on the phone until it was time for bed. We talked about every possibility, prayed, cried, and he assured me that I would be okay. He always believed that we would be okay no matter what the circumstances were. Even when I struggled to get pregnant, we would pray, and he would tell me that God would make it happen. When I didn't have faith, he had faith for me (not in me, but for me). I believed him and went to sleep that night after we prayed.

The Diagnosis

I did not want to inform anyone else that I was at the hospital. I felt lonely, but I managed to deal with it. The next morning, my husband called to inquire about the test results. I told him to go to work and that I would call him when I was ready to be discharged. I spent the time scrolling through social media on my phone. At around 9:30 am, my doctor entered the room with another doctor whom he introduced as an oncologist. I did not understand why an oncologist was visiting me because I thought they only treated cancer patients. I was expecting to hear that I had miscarried and could be discharged.

The oncologist, however, informed me that I had choriocarcinoma, a form of cancer that originates in the uterus and has spread to my lungs and brain. I was stunned and could not cry. I could not believe that this was happening to me. The oncologist drew a diagram on the board to help me understand what was happening. I noticed that the nurse who had been assisting me all night had tears in her eyes. I thought that I was going to die.

After the oncologist explained everything, he asked if I had any questions. I had a million questions, but my first was whether I was going to die. He did not give me the answer I was hoping for. He said that we would start with emergency surgery to remove the tumors. I wanted to know how many tumors there were and why they had not been detected during my vaginal ultrasound a month earlier. The oncologist did not answer my questions. He looked hurt and sad. He looked like he wanted to cry. I could tell that he knew he had made a mistake and was remorseful. The oncologist was usually very outgoing and cheerful, but this time he was different. He had scheduled a hysterectomy for the next day because the cancer was spreading. He looked at me with an expression that said, "I am sorry," but the words never came out. He hugged me and left the room. He did not say whether I was going to be okay. I assumed that I was dying.

After the oncologist left, I sat there for about an hour, trying to figure out how I would tell my husband, parents, siblings, and friends. I did not know if I should call my parents first or my husband. I thought about not telling my parents because they live in Miami, Florida, and I did not want to upset them. My father had been diagnosed with prostate cancer ten years earlier, and I thought that if I got better without them knowing, it would be okay. I would just avoid visiting them for a while. My thoughts were racing.

I decided to call my husband first. He answered the phone and asked, "What did the doctor say?" I started to cry. He asked, "What's going on?" I told him that the doctor had said that I had cancer. I hung up the phone and cried into my pillow. I looked up and saw my husband standing in the doorway with flowers, balloons, and other gifts. He must have arrived immediately after I hung up the phone. Thirty minutes later, my brother-in-law and sister-in-law arrived. It seemed like they had all appeared by magic. Everyone had left work early to be with me. Having my family with me was comforting, but I still felt alone. I was the one who was going through this, and no one else could understand what I was going through.

As I was discussing my condition with my family, the doctor walked in, which was an excellent opportunity to ask questions and for my family to ask the questions they were unable to ask before. First, he inquired whether it was acceptable for him to speak in front of everyone. I replied in the affirmative because they were the only family I had in Nashville. I introduced everyone to him, and he continued to explain his plans for me. He informed us that I was scheduled to have another CT scan of my brain and that the following day, I would have surgery for a hysterectomy. After surgery, I would remain in the hospital for another five days to receive another surgery to insert a port in my chest for my chemotherapy treatments. He stated that chemotherapy was the best option for my type of cancer and that if it were successful, I would be fine.

There, I heard that I would be fine if the chemotherapy was successful. I wanted to be reassured that I would be okay. But that's if it works. I know that it will work because God will heal me, and I know that God will not allow me to leave my then two-year-old son without a mother. My family was incredibly supportive that day, and I needed them. I am grateful for them.

While conversing and joking with the family, my phone rang, and it was my sister from Miami inquiring about how the procedure had gone. I had forgotten that I had told my family I was having a DNC to stop the bleeding and clotting. She called, so I had to tell her. My heart sank. I informed her that I had not undergone the procedure and that the doctor had instead discovered cancer. I heard her exclaim, "WHAT?" I told her to inform our parents. I didn't want to be the one to tell them.

My mother called me back immediately. I could hear her voice trembling. She said that I would be fine, and that God would heal me. I believed her. I told her she didn't have to come because I was fine. She handed my father the phone, and he wanted me to explain to him what the doctor had told me. I told him everything, and he didn't say much, but I know how much my father loves and worries about me. He said they would do everything they could to ensure I was healed. Growing up with Haitian parents, I already knew that they meant natural remedies in addition to chemotherapy, changing my diet, and more.

I began to think about what I had done wrong to cause cancer. I couldn't think of anything. That afternoon, I was scheduled to have a CT scan of my brain, and I remember it like it was yesterday. I remember waiting in the room for the nurse to take me to the scan room, and when the nurse arrived, my husband and I were praying in the room. We were lying in the bed when the nurse told my husband that she was taking me to get a CT scan. My husband got up from the bed, and we still held hands as the nurse started to roll me while I was still in the bed. We continued to pray. We prayed that the scan would show no signs of cancer in my brain, that I would be completely healed, and that I would make a speedy recovery. During the scan, I was nervous, but I was ready to hear the results and begin my treatment process. When I came out of the room, my husband was waiting outside the door, and he said, "This is just a small setback, and everything will be okay." His faith has always been strong.

The next day, my oncologist came in with my test results and assured me that there was no cancer in my brain. He seemed surprised, as if he had thought it would be in my brain, but my husband and I had already prayed, and I believed that God had taken care of it. As the doctor explained my test results, he also prepared me for my surgery the next morning. He gave me a detailed explanation of what to expect before and after the surgery. He assured me that the surgery would go well and that it would be the beginning of my healing process. The oncologist seemed like a good person. He was patient, and I could tell that he enjoyed his job. He made me feel very comfortable. I really liked his demeanor.

Surgery Day

I woke up that morning feeling nervous, but also ready for the surgery. When I entered the operating room, I was met by a team of people who I didn't know, but I had a feeling they were going to take good care of me.

After the surgery, I woke up in a different room with flowers, cards, balloons, and a lot of pain. I looked around and saw my brother-in-law and a nurse. He had moved all my belongings to my new room, which I would be in for the next seven days. It was the first time I had felt hungry in three days, as I had lost my appetite after the surgery. But on this day, I was able to eat. I think that after having the surgery, it was a relief to know it had gone well.

Later that day, the hospital room was crowded with visitors, and I was grateful to have so many people who cared about me. But the very next day, reality began to sink in that I would never be able to get pregnant again. I cried because I didn't realize how much I wanted more children until after the surgery. It felt like my body was failing me, and I was powerless to do anything about it. I started to think about how, as a woman, I could no longer reproduce, and it was painful. I was hurt. I was ready to get the surgery over with, but I didn't think it would affect me the way that it did. Even if I didn't want a child right away, my heart would have been pleased and happy if I had another child. The thought really hurt. I spoke to my mom about it, and she said, "Your healing is a lot more important, and you can always adopt a baby."

I spent several days in the hospital after my surgery, and I had to undergo one more surgery before I was able to go home. This was to insert a port in my chest for chemotherapy. After the port was inserted, I stayed in the hospital for another three days. What was supposed to be an outpatient procedure turned into a ten-day hospital stay. We never know what tomorrow will bring, and our plans can change at any moment. We must embrace it and keep pushing no matter the outcome. I learned that quickly.

After leaving the hospital, I went home and realized that I was powerless. I couldn't function the way I wanted to. I couldn't go up and down the stairs, I couldn't lift my son up for a hug, I couldn't stand for too long, and when I coughed, it was extremely painful. I couldn't lay down on my stomach the way I used to. Everything was different, and my life was changing. I wanted everything to return to normal, but I knew it wouldn't.

In a couple of weeks, I would be starting chemotherapy, and that thought was scary. I was researching everything about it, wanting to know about every side effect, if it was painful, if I would be sick, and if it would kill me. Everything I researched was a yes. I was having severe anxiety, but I didn't want to tell anyone. I prayed harder than I ever had before.

First Chemotherapy

I could not sleep the night before chemotherapy day. It was not a surprise that I watched documentaries all night on chemotherapy. I woke up early because I was told I would be in the hospital for three days. It was a Wednesday morning. I had everything packed. I hugged, kissed, and squeezed my son, then dropped him off at daycare. My friend Linda took me to chemotherapy that morning because I told my husband to go to work and come by after work. While in the car, I called a few friends who were out of state, and we talked and prayed. I received great devotion that day from family and friends. Linda and I stopped at my favorite breakfast place for a sandwich and coffee before arriving at the hospital.

Once we arrived, I was assigned a room on the chemo floor. The nurse spoke to me and explained the process. The nurse gave me what looked like a book to sign, which basically said that chemotherapy could kill me, that my family could not sue them, and that I agreed to do it. I signed it because I wanted to heal and be better; I wanted to be around for my son.

Since it was my very first chemotherapy treatment, the process was a bit different. As I mentioned before, I had to be admitted for three days to receive intensive treatment. I remember two nurses entering the room; one nurse inserted the needle into my port, and the second nurse got the medicine ready. My oncologist walked into the room, to my surprise, because I did not expect to see him that day. The nurses and he went over a few things that the nurse had already mentioned. I remember him saying that if I felt like I was burning, unable to breathe, if I felt like an elephant was sitting on my chest, or if I felt like I was going to faint, please raise my hand if I couldn't speak and if I could speak, tell them right away. All I could answer back was, "Okay." I said a quick, silent prayer and asked God to heal me and be my medicine.

The nurse was dressed as if she was going to space. Usually, hospital nurses wear scrubs, a mask, and gloves, but these two nurses were chemotherapy-certified. I asked why they looked like astronauts (jokingly), because I wanted something to distract me, and one replied that it was standard procedure because if the treatment were to leak and fall on their skin, it would burn them. I was thinking, "Wow," but this burning solution or poison was going into my body. I never said anything and replied, "Okay."

The first medicine given to me was an anti-nausea medicine. The nurse said it would prevent me from throwing up and being too sick after chemo. It was given to me for about ten minutes. I could hear the beeping sound once it was done. It was really fast, and after five minutes, I was ready for the real thing. The nurse proceeded to replace the bag with the chemo medicine. I was watching both nurses and everything they were doing. She asked if I was ready, and I replied, "Yes." While the meds started dripping, both nurses stood there and were staring at me for at least ten to fifteen minutes. After another five minutes, they smiled at each other and said, "Well, she's handling it well, and she's doing pretty good." One of the nurses left. I asked the nurse in the room what she meant by "she's handling it well." She replied that my body was doing well with the treatment and that it was the toughest treatment I would be getting each week. I was a bit more relaxed after the nurse confirmed that I was doing good. But I was still nervous.

I received treatment that day and for the next three days, and I felt fine. I thought this was a piece of cake, it wasn't too bad, and I should be back to normal life in a few days. I went home that Friday evening and thought this was a breeze and chemotherapy wasn't so bad.

The following day, on Saturday, I attempted to get out of bed. However, walking the short distance to the bathroom felt like climbing a mountain. I was dizzy, nauseous, and in pain, but I didn't know what was causing it. Was it muscular pain? Bone pain? I felt uncomfortable and unlike anything I had ever felt before. I felt almost paralyzed and began to wonder if the hospital had given me too much treatment. I was weak and didn't know how I would make it through the weeks and months of treatment to come.

My brother-in-law and sister-in-law were planning their wedding, and I was one of their bridesmaids. With the wedding only a few weeks away, I was worried that I wouldn't be able to attend because I could barely stand. After weeks of treatment, my body began to adjust to the treatment, and I had more energy. However, I was still extremely tired. The week of the wedding, I was in the hospital for treatment and was released on Friday, the day before the wedding. That evening, I attended the rehearsal dinner. It was a welcome distraction from my health. Being around family and friends and thinking about the wedding brought me joy and helped me forget about my cancer for a short while.

On my sister's wedding day, I woke up early to get my hair done. When I arrived at the salon, my hair was coming out in clumps. I was devastated. I knew that it would eventually fall out due to the chemotherapy, but I had hoped that it would wait until after the wedding. The stylist shaved my head, and I was in tears. I didn't want to look bald at my sister's wedding. I didn't want anyone to look at me and think that I was sick. I went to a few wig stores, but nothing looked right. I was angry and upset that I was going to ruin my family's wedding. Eventually, I went to a jewelry store and found some jewelry that I could wear on my head. It wasn't ideal, but it was the best I could do. Most people didn't even realize that I was going through cancer or that my hair had fallen out due to chemotherapy. They all thought that I had just shaved my head. I received compliment after compliment from strangers, which was surprising and uplifting.

Weeks and months passed, and I was still undergoing chemotherapy. I started to do some research about uterine cancer and was surprised to find out how little information was available. I thought that more awareness should be raised about this type of cancer. I am not usually one to seek out public attention, but I started posting more on social media about uterine cancer and my journey. I also started a blog to raise awareness about the disease. After a few weeks, I began receiving messages from people all over the world asking me about uterine cancer. Seeing that my story resonated with others was both shocking and exciting.

During my time at chemotherapy, I met other patients who were also going through cancer treatment. Some of them stopped coming to treatment, and we didn't know what happened to them. It was scary not knowing what their status was. One of the patients told me that she sometimes missed her treatments because she didn't have a way to get there. I started providing her with free transportation, and we talked about other patients who needed the same help. After a few months, I started a nonprofit organization to provide free services to cancer patients. At the time, our services included free transportation, groceries, and support groups. We also provided wigs to patients who couldn't afford them.

The Nonprofit Organization

The nonprofit is called The TeamCJColas Uterine Cancer Foundation, a 501(c)(3) nonprofit organization committed to providing comprehensive support services to cancer patients and their families. Our mission is to improve the quality of life for those affected by cancer by offering a range of free services and resources.

Our Services Include:

Free Transportation to Treatment Centers: We offer free transportation assistance to ensure cancer patients can access their necessary medical appointments without added stress or financial burden.

Free Childcare Services: We provide free childcare services to alleviate the childcare responsibilities of cancer patients undergoing treatment, allowing them to focus on their health and recovery.

Free Wigs: We offer free wigs to help cancer patients cope with the physical changes that may result from cancer treatment, promoting self-esteem and confidence.

Free Support Groups: Our foundation hosts support groups where patients can connect with others facing similar challenges, share experiences, and receive emotional support.

Free Educational Workshops: We organize educational workshops to empower patients with knowledge about uterine cancer, treatment options, and self-care practices.

Free Summer Program: Our organization offers a complimentary summer program for children whose families are dealing with cancer and other serious medical conditions. This initiative aims to alleviate the concerns of parents and families undergoing treatment, who may struggle to find suitable arrangements for their children during the summer months.

We are always looking for community partners who share our commitment to supporting individuals affected by cancer. We would love to connect with you and learn how my work can support your organization. Please do not hesitate to reach out.

Today, our nonprofit has served over 450 cancer patients in less than four years. We provide a variety of services, including free transportation to and from treatment centers, free wigs, free support groups, free childcare for patients undergoing chemotherapy, free summer programs for cancer families, holiday drives, and health fairs. We are still growing and looking for ways to offer more services. We have many goals, and we want to see cancer patients worry less from the time of diagnosis to remission. For more information about our nonprofit, please visit our website at www.teamcjcolas.org.

In essence, reflecting on the factors that have shaped my life and led me to where I am today involves a careful examination of my life choices, experiences, and the role that life itself has played in my journey. This reflection can yield valuable insight into my personal growth and development, as well as the lessons I have learned from the experiences that have shaped my life.

Cancer wasn't the end of my journey. It was just the start to a new life. My journey is just beginning.

CJ Colas

ABOUT THE AUTHOR - CJ COLAS

CJ Colas is a uterine cancer warrior. She is a mother to a Blessing that she waited to receive from God for many years and the wife to the most wonderful man who has honored her throughout their marriage and supported her in every way possible.

CJ is a college graduate and an entrepreneur who loves spending time with her family. She moved to Nashville with her husband a few years ago from Miami, FL, where she had lived her entire life. Leaving her family and friends was hard, but it was a great decision that led her to many great things in Nashville.

In August 2016, she was diagnosed with stage 4 uterine cancer, and by the time the physician gave her the news, it had spread to her lungs. She had to undergo an emergency surgery (hysterectomy) to prevent the cancer from spreading further. Currently, CJ is in remission, but during her treatment journey, she created The TeamCJColas Uterine Cancer Foundation, a 501 (c)(3) nonprofit organization to bring awareness to Uterine Cancer and create resources for women who are fighting cancer with no support.

Her foundation consists of helping patients to and from treatment centers, free support groups, free summer programs for cancer families, educational workshops, free childcare support for cancer families, and more. It also creates quarterly screenings for women, mental and physical needs, and most importantly, it brings awareness to the communities that lack knowledge of uterine cancer.

CHAPTER THREE
THE NOT SO SHRINKING VIOLET
DR. KIMBERLY GOLDEN

DEDICATION

To my Lord and Savior, Jesus Christ, I cannot thank you enough. I could write volumes on your love alone. Through it all, I knew you were always for me. There would be no me without you. Thank you for love, patience, forgiveness, mercy, and grace. Thank you for never giving up on me. You are my rock, my friend, my love, my everything! I owe you my all.

To my "heartbeats," Angelica Golden, Arielle Golden, and Andrew Golden. You are my inspiration and my reason for every breath I take. You are my biggest WHY for everything I aspire to accomplish in this world. I love you immeasurably, and I thank God for you. I am in awe of you and am your biggest fan! God intricately designed each of you with undeniable purpose, grace, favor, and resilience. I'm so proud of you. You literally light up my entire world. I hope you glean knowledge from my missteps as well as my triumphs. My prayer is that you will never shrink, nor dull your shine. You are authentic. You are powerful. You are enough, and you are simply amazing!

To my grandangels, Jayden, Ariyonna, Laylah, Jaielle, Khalil, and Kobe (who's on the way), you are my legacy. I see my children in your eyes, and it feels amazing just to hold you in my arms. You are blessings from above. I pray you will always dream big and soar beyond all perceived limitations. May you always serve God and live in divine purpose. And may you prosper in all! Nana loves you so much!

To my mom, Deborah McAdoo, thank you for simply being boldly beautiful. I appreciate your praying hands, your sweet voice, your wisdom, tenacity, joy, and creative genius. There is always a song in your heart that ministers to mine. You are a gift. I love you so much more than you know!

To my dad, Bishop Brent Bryant, thank you for always showing up as the epitome of godliness, grace, masculinity, and love. I appreciate your wisdom, your big heart, your laughter, and your support. Your impact is far-reaching, and I admire the man and the leader that you are. I love you very, very much!

To Memaw and Poppy in Heaven, thank you for everything. There was no measure to your unconditional love. You are forever etched in my heart, and I carry you with me always. I hope, in some small way, I've made you proud. You left a beautiful legacy with memories to cherish forever. I miss and love you with my whole heart.

To Grandma and Grandpa Wyatt in Heaven, I miss you and love you. Thank you for your godly example and character. I can still taste Grandma's caramel cake and homemade ice cream! Memories of you make me smile.

To all of my siblings, Marquetta Broady, Sherry McAdoo, Sherrell Bryant, Tonya McAdoo-Moore, Marvin Briggs, Naphtali Bryant, Brent "Kool" Bryant, and Adrian Merriweather (gone but never forgotten), I love you all!

Dr. Tanya Davis, Thank you for this opportunity. You exude femininity, beauty, strength, and grace. You are truly a Queen who ROCKS!

"THE NOT SO SHRINKING VIOLET"
DR. KIMBERLY GOLDEN

*Disclaimer ** The story told below is the author's version of life events as they took place. The author recognizes that other people's memories of the events described in the book may differ from her own. The details are not intended to hurt, defame, or offend anyone.*

I am beautifully and authentically adorned in the most radiant, captivating purple. Aesthetically, I appear small, but there is an air of distinct royalty as I sway rhythmically amongst the garden. My delicate fragrance tantalizes butterflies, as my nectar's medicinal prowess can stimulate healing within mankind, pleasing the senses. I freely dance in the wind with reckless abandonment, as my heart-shaped leaves arouse man's desire for love and romance. I am coy, but I surrender to the mating call. My roots extend to the deepest parts of Mother Earth. I can feel her vibration calling me to reproduce. Her wish is granted as my posterity multiplies with breathtaking regalia. I extend my leaves to the sun in gentle gratitude. That is until I spotted the rose.

Oh, that beautiful rose! Donned in crimson red, she was striking! She commanded the attention of all the flowers in the garden and all passersby. The wind could not regulate her dance as she dug her roots into the ground. Her petals were kissed by the sun. The bees drew nectar from her, but she never swayed, nor did she succumb to their stings. Her presence was so powerful! She was a star amongst flowers. Her stem was girded with thorns that warded off any who sought to pluck her. I longed to be more like her. I admired her fortitude, her confidence, and her charisma. How could such a petite violet stand in the presence of such a rose? That was the first time I began to shrink.

My mother is the most exquisite rose. A standout amongst others, her petals glisten in vibrant orange. She blossoms to the beat of her own music emanating from her stem. She is distinctively positioned in the center of the garden, inviting the rays of the sun to highlight her luminescence. She stands boldly with grace and beauty.

I basked in my mother's wisdom as she once gently said to me, "You are like a shrinking violet. You have so much within you, but you tend to shrink in public. You must stand up and be noticed. You have what it takes to do whatever you want to do." I embraced her words and began my journey of introspection. I was unaware that my private limiting beliefs were manifested in my public demeanor. I was blessed with a plethora of visions and dreams. Since one of my deepest desires was to be an instrument of healing to women and young ladies, I had to begin with myself.

I began with a courageous visit to memories I had buried within the deepest recesses of my heart and mind. Do you have any secrets buried within? I had several…and for many years. One of those secrets was the little girl imprisoned within my soul. This little girl cried in the dark and had multiple nightmares. She was very timid in public and afraid to speak her truth. She had strived to be the good little girl that her family would be proud of. Her fear of failure and her desire to earn love led to perfectionistic habits, people-pleasing behaviors, overachieving tendencies, and self-punishment. That little girl was me. I carried her broken soul within my spirit for years.

As you read further, I must disclose that my story may be triggering for some. I encourage you to please seek the counsel of a licensed therapist to help guide you through your healing process. My prayer is that my story will help you unveil yours and lead you to a place where you will no longer live in the shadows, shrinking within. This is your invitation to begin your journey.

When I was about four or five years old, a family friend's daughter used to babysit me. Once the adults left the house, she would reach for my extensive collection of Barbie dolls and begin to role-play. She let me play with some of the Barbies, but she always made me play with a Ken doll, too. Most little girls enjoyed dressing their Barbie dolls in fancy clothes and pretending they would get married and have big homes and nice cars. But my babysitter always made us play out a soap opera scenario of my Ken doll cheating on her Barbie. The scenes would be so realistic to her that she would often shed real tears as my Ken would be apologizing to her Barbie. In the midst of this scene, she tearfully forgives Ken and proceeds to "make up" by molesting me. This happened every single time she babysat me, which was quite often on weekends. As I reflect on it today, perhaps she was mimicking the scenes of what was happening in her personal life. But I was much too young to relate.

She would make me promise not to tell anyone, instilling fear in me by stating that if I told anyone, my parents would be very angry with ME. She said they would be so ashamed of what WE had done. She sealed the deal with guilt by explaining how I would also get her into so much trouble if I ever said anything to anyone. Then, she would "reward" me with treats. I never said a word. But one day, I received some news that would ultimately set me free. We were a military family, and we were being sent overseas to live for three years. I cannot articulate the level of relief I felt. We were leaving, and I would never have to face her again. Or so I thought.

Within the third year of living overseas, I was told her family had moved to the same country on the same base. How could this happen? I smiled on the outside but shrank horribly on the inside. But this time was different. By this time, I was approximately nine years old. She sat in my room and told me she would not do to me now what she had done in the past. She strongly cautioned me again about telling anyone, saying I would still get into a lot of trouble if I did. She even apologized to me.

I guess for some, that might have been closure. But I was too young to process any of it alone. She had planted numerous seeds of shame, powerlessness, manipulation, and low self-esteem within my soul. Her apology was like a band-aid over multiple stab wounds. I kept bleeding.

Today, I look at my grandchildren, and I see how vulnerable they are at such young ages. I wonder how anyone could have looked at my underdeveloped body at that age with eyes of lust. What would life have been like if I had grown up with the same innocence I saw in the eyes of my grandchildren? When I was a little girl, I could not even sit comfortably in a family member's lap like other little girls did without feeling some measure of caution and alarm. The seeds that were planted by the babysitter germinated in my developing soul and established roots that grew into a system of internal weeds.

The roots of shrinking violets run deep. As such, I have read many studies and have heard many behavioral health practitioners state that childhood sexual abuse may result in various disorders, including possible changes in the shape or size of specific parts of the brain. That is why it is so important to seek assistance from a licensed professional, coupled with much prayer. You are worth the investment.

I wish I could tell you the abuse ended with the babysitter. But that was only the beginning. I was twelve years old and in seventh grade. Our football team was about to play against a rival school. I met a cute boy at the game with a long Jheri curl. So, let's call him "Jheri." We started talking on the phone daily, and I was enamored!

One day, we strategically planned how we would secretly meet at a park. Once we got there, he asked me to walk with him to his home. I was a little nervous, but I felt safe because his uncle was sitting in the living room when we arrived at his home. He and I went upstairs to his room. I had never been alone with a boy before. He talked to me for a few minutes and then leaned over to kiss me. Then he touched me. The touches progressed. That's when I told him to stop...repeatedly. He refused.

Instead, to my horror, he grabbed a gun from his jacket and pointed it. He then put the gun down and began to rape me. I loudly screamed for help, hoping his uncle would run upstairs and rescue me. He never came. Because I was a virgin, the task was extremely difficult for Jheri, so after a while, he seemed to get tired of trying. Finally, he stopped, frustrated that he couldn't finish because I kept moving and screaming. He threatened to harm my family if I told anyone. Again, I felt powerless. To add insult to injury, his uncle was still sitting in the living room when we walked back downstairs. He stared coldly at the television and avoided any measure of eye contact with me as I walked right in front of him to leave.

Once I returned home, I faced serious trouble for sneaking off to be with Jheri. I remained silent through all of the reprimands and talks of how disappointed everyone was in my actions. After school, Jheri would still call me and often ask me if I told anyone. I told him I had not, but he continued to threaten to harm my parents. Most days after school, I would peep outside to see if he was out there, afraid he might be watching. I lived in fear for weeks. I also became progressively sick...daily.

The pregnancy test was positive. I had barely reached my thirteenth birthday. How could I be pregnant? He said he never finished when he raped me, so I thought all of this was over. I was devastated and baffled. Within a short time, decisions had been made on my behalf as a minor in my best interest, and I was taken to a clinic.

I was tearful and afraid. The nurse gave me Valium to relax me. It put me to sleep. When the effects of the Valium wore off, they called my name. The room was very cold, small, and sterile. The doctor was less than reassuring and seemed to be in a hurry. He tried to use instruments to access my cervix, but the pain was unbearable. I cried and could not relax despite several prompts from the nurses. The doctor seemed quite irritated at my reluctance, most likely because of their assumptions, not knowing that my pregnancy had been a result of force.

When the procedure was over, I felt hurt, shame, guilt, and numbness. I believe I remained numb inside for years. A person can smile on the outside but feel empty inside. I moved on with life, unhealed and unwell. It took me years to realize I needed additional help. I had read books about healing from molestation and rape. Through prayer, journaling, and inner work, I actually felt better. But there were still a few patterns that had manifested in my life. In the church, we refer to those as strongholds.

As such, I entered verbally and physically abusive relationships, relationships with men who demonstrated narcissistic type behaviors, relationships in which I was disrespected, and relationships that subtracted from me. In each new relationship, I strived to make better choices. I'm not saying that every man had something wrong with him. What I am saying is that it was the same cycle but with different manifestations. I had to accept that the common denominator was me. To make matters worse, very little of this was private, so the root of shame inside me was choking the mess out of me! And some were beginning to say unkind and judgmental things.

One thing I realized is that I could not allow myself to get stuck in a victim mentality. Let me be clear…yes, there were things that happened TO me, especially as a child. But as I grew older, I learned to accept accountability for my own missteps, such as ignoring red flags, people pleasing, and not taking care of myself. When you find yourself enduring toxic patterns in your life, please take inventory, pray, and seek guidance. The truth may lend itself as unpalatable medicine, but if you will ingest truth consistently and apply it to your life, it will be for your betterment. You can fly so much higher when the weight is lifted from your wings. Free yourself, sisters. You are worth fighting for.

As a footnote, have you ever shared your dysfunctional relationship story with a trusted girlfriend only to have her tell you, "Giiiirrrrl, you're a good one, because I would have --!" When you're a shrinking violet, you may laugh a little when a rose gives you that type of feedback, but you shrink a little internally due to the embarrassment of possibly being viewed as weak or foolish. After all, the rose would never tolerate the things you endured. Those thoughts played on repeat in my mind. That shame led to anger with myself because I wasn't as formidable as roses in my life.

Comparison is an antagonist to progress. The roses are not your competition. It's you versus you! The only healthy comparison is reviewing your past personal progress so you can determine your next steps toward your goals and dreams. Comparison is a trap. It either feeds your pride or your low self-esteem. As for me, comparison magnified my personal feelings of inadequacy. I was frustrated with myself. I know I'm not the only one who's looked in the mirror and asked, "What's wrong with you, and why can't you get it together?" But what happens when anger is turned inward? Depression. I masked that for many years and all too well. I knew how to show up in public with big smiles on deck. But I was lost when it was time to show up for myself.

Over time, I grew weary of trying to do it all by myself. I realized I needed help, so I prayed and sought the counsel of a licensed professional. One of my best friends supported that decision and even sought counsel for herself. Quite frankly, I was stunned at her decision because she was the last person I thought would need help. She was the most successful and distinctive rose I had ever met in my life. I thought she had it ALL together. That taught me a valuable lesson. Never judge a rose by her petals. Every rose, well…every flower has a story. You are not alone.

I went to therapy, did the work, and things were improving. I experienced success in my career, my finances, my credit, and my family. I had three amazing offspring that I refer to as "my heartbeats" and had begun to be blessed with the most beautiful "grandangels" on this side of heaven! I felt much better about myself, though I understood I still had more work to do. I hope that encourages you because healing is a process. Be patient with yourself and embrace the journey. It can lead you to a tranquil space where you discover your truths and begin to fall more in love with yourself.

That's exactly what was happening to me. It was sublime! But when you are on your journey, there will be occasional, yet very strategic, pitfalls along your path. The pitfalls are not the issue. The issue is whether you are able to discern and identify those pitfalls before you take the next step, sign the next deal, or enter into the next relationship. That's where I stumbled. I met a friend. My friend was an entrepreneur who boasted abundant confidence in the ability to secure their dream. Before I knew it, I was sold!

I freely invested and continued to invest beyond my capacity. Has your heart ever led you to say yes to what your spirit is screaming no to? I ignored the screams and went all in. I convinced myself that the return on investment would surely happen within the year. I listened to the reassuring words my friend rehearsed daily in my ears. I had not practiced the one sentence that could have saved me a ton of regret, which was simply, "NO." The word "no" carries a whole lot of weight and power. Use it! I wish I had because a few months later, on one fateful evening, I received a phone call that shook my entire world.

I cannot share details, but I promise it felt like a scene from the movie, "Crash." In one instant, BOOM! There I was, alone…shouldering a boatload of debt, coupled with a completely drained financial portfolio and a zero return on investment. I was literally catapulted back to square one. I couldn't even be mad at my friend because I had jumped willingly into that pit. I lost my finances, my peace, my confidence, my trust in myself, and my joy. And yes, shame was more than happy to oblige as the shrinking violet emerged.

I was angry with myself again. To add insult to injury, I had just recently begun training as a brand-new financial services professional. Yet I had made a complete mess of my own finances with one unwise decision rooted in my own limiting beliefs. Have you ever embarked on a business journey but got in your own way because you felt unqualified, unequipped, and undeserving? It's called imposter syndrome. I was the poster child for it. How could I help others with their finances when I had made such an incredible mess of my own? I spent months in disillusionment and seclusion at home with just me and God. This was my rock bottom. I had to rest, reflect, regroup, and recover.

During that season of my life, I learned to give myself grace as I gleaned lessons with gratitude. There are many multimillionaires who have stories of losing everything but gaining it all back, plus more! If you have invested unwisely, or simply loved and lost, be encouraged. You can recover it all. And I know a God who can MULTIPLY it back to you.

This is one of many reasons why I do what I do as a financial services professional. My career actually began in healthcare. I still love holistic healthcare, as I love how God created our bodies with self-repair mechanisms that often just need a little help through nutrition and lifestyle changes. I never thought that one day I would help individuals with financial education to assist them in building wealth and establishing generational wealth for their families. In my late teens, my grandfather tried to talk to me about budgeting, and I ran from those conversations! I laugh about that now. I always told God I wanted to be an extension of His Hands. I believe I am that extension now, as I still offer health coaching in partnership with an incredible functional medicine provider, Dr. Jermaine Ware. But I now realize why my career in financial services is more than a business. It's a ministry.

Stress can be significantly harmful to the body. It can lead to diseases and dysfunction in the body and amplify underlying conditions. Stress increases cortisol in the body, which can lead to residual harmful effects. What is one of the primary stressors for many individuals and families?

Finances! Even marriages are often negatively impacted by financial woes, resulting in high rates of divorce. When I educate and help individuals and families with their finances, I am also most likely helping to alleviate stress, which can lead to improved health outcomes. What a blessing!

We are living in challenging times, but it's also a time during which there is a window of opportunity to change the trajectory of your financial future and the financial futures of your children and generations to come. There are those who argue that we should not focus on finances. I agree that finances should not be our number one focus, but it should be included on our top priority list. The Bible states in Ecclesiastes 10:19 that money answers all things. Whether you believe in the Bible or not, most would agree. It is not all things. It ANSWERS all things. For example, there are medical breakthroughs that would not even be discovered if it were not for the money spent on research and development. That is just one example. What problems could you resolve within your own family if you had more money? What issues could you resolve in your community if you had money to give?

There are underlying beliefs and behaviors that can potentially lead to financial poverty. For example, there are those who assert it is wrong to possess large sums of money. They believe that a poverty mindset is somehow linked to righteousness. Then there are some (oftentimes women) who spend money emotionally. When they experience feelings of sadness or anxiousness, they spend to numb the pain. This spending often creates a temporary sense of euphoria. Many are chronic consumers with no retirement savings and no emergency fund. Some of these misnomers and behaviors result from limiting beliefs, past wounds, unresolved psychological issues, and miseducation. Others are a direct reflection of learned behaviors from their parents or caregivers.

Hosea 4:6 states, *"My people are destroyed for lack of knowledge.* Many of us were not properly educated about finances. We were taught to go to college, work a job, put money in the bank, and perhaps create a budget. Because we were not taught how to manage money, build wealth, build our credit, or diversify our financial portfolios, many continue to perpetuate cycles of debt with little to no understanding of how to strategically save or increase their savings for retirement, nor how to protect their assets and families properly. Many have entered retirement only to outlive their retirement funds. Sadly, they are financially compelled to reenter the workforce and work well beyond the average retirement age.

I have witnessed families desperately resorting to the use of crowdfunding sources for personal fundraising to secure funds to bury an unprotected loved one. Women, in particular, are disproportionately lacking life insurance coverage. According to an article in Forbes published in 2024, women are twice as likely to lack life insurance coverage compared to men. This is a disturbing statistic.

Life insurance is not solely about a death benefit. Life insurance can be used to help with financial security for the surviving spouse and children, pay off remaining debts, pay off funeral expenses, and, in some cases, even provide living benefits if the insured becomes critically, chronically, or terminally ill. There are types of permanent life insurance that can also be used for tax-advantaged savings, but please consult with a licensed professional, such as myself, before deciding which plans to choose.

I am neither a tax accountant nor a financial advisor; therefore, I am not a replacement for either. I am a financial professional who can strategically educate you on ways to diversify and increase your savings, adequately protect yourself and your family, and plan your legacy to protect your assets and your children in the event of your passing.

This is why I educate families on at least three rules of money. One of those rules is the Rule of 72. This rule helps you better understand the accumulation phase of your money. This is an important rule to grasp as it will help you make wiser financial decisions when determining how to best save and grow your money. It is a calculation that helps you determine how long your money will take to double one time in an account based on the interest rate. The calculation is simple. Divide the percent interest rate of your account into 72, and the result will show approximately how many years it will take your money to double one time in that account. For example, let's say the interest rate on your account is 6%. Divide 72 by 6, and your answer is 12. So, if the interest rate on your account remains 6% and you do not withdraw any of the funds from that account, your money should double in that account once in year 12. If you keep your money in that account at the same interest rate indefinitely with no changes, your money will most likely double every twelve years.

In contrast, do you believe there would be a significant difference if your money is in an account with a 1% interest rate? Let's see! Divide 72 by 1, and your answer is 72. In this account, if the interest rate remains at 1% and you don't take money out of it, your money would most likely double ONE TIME in year 72! Are you satisfied with waiting 72 years for your money to double in your account once? If not, we need to chat!

Historically, women and minorities have been underrepresented in the financial services industry. It excites me that STEM programs target young girls and minorities to increase their interest in math, science, and more. As an independent professional, I strive to make a difference by educating families and attracting, training, and grooming more females and minorities into this rewarding field. I am passionate about this as it is imperative for females and minority communities to receive financial education and apply it for the betterment and progress of these communities. However, financial education is necessary for all, and I offer it to all.

In my meetings with individuals, I cannot count how many times I've heard them say, "I wish I knew all of this a long time ago." I can relate because I felt the same way when I learned the rules of money. If I had known what I know now years ago, my children would have had a promising financial trajectory by the time they graduated from high school. Based on what I know today, I believe they would have been well established on a path to a minimum of seven figures by the time they retired. But as a "Nana," I am planting those seeds for my "grandangels." Our family's last name will be changed, and generational chains will be broken, beginning with me. One of my greatest goals is to leave a legacy for my children and my children's children. But my vision doesn't stop with me and my family. It extends to you and yours as well.

In conclusion, I am blessed to say that this formerly shrinking violet is standing taller these days. By the grace of God, I found my voice and my purpose. I have discovered much joy in my alone times with God through my journey. I can share that joy with my family. I am much more appreciative and intentional with creating beautiful memories. One of my greatest lessons is that I don't have to become a rose to be worthy. I've discovered the value of being a violet, and I rock it! Some violets are purple. Purple is associated with royalty, dignity, and power. Violets are delicate and feminine, but their roots are grounded. And

God cares for the violets just as well as He cares for the roses.

My dance is authentic and unashamed as I sway with the wind and bathe in sun rays unapologetically amongst all the flowers, including the beautiful roses. I'm not afraid of the storms anymore because I trust God and am learning to trust myself. When I see roses, I celebrate them as I celebrate myself. I applaud every flower because we are all fearfully and wonderfully made!

Beautiful Queens, whether you identify as a violet, a rose, a lily, a sunflower, or whatever flower you resonate with…let us all dance collectively in our varied array of colors and splendor! You are worthy. You are loved for who you are. You are unique. You are powerful. You are special. You are beautiful. You are gifted. You are simply phenomenal. No matter what you've been through or what you've done, don't you ever shrink! Stand tall in your uniqueness, authenticity, and grace. Never give up on you. Embrace your process and take hold of what you need to assist you along the way. You deserve it. Why? Because YOU ROCK!

ABOUT THE AUTHOR - DR. KIMBERLY GOLDEN

Dr. Kimberly Golden is a remarkable individual with a diverse range of accomplishments. She dedicates her life to positively impacting individuals, families, and communities. Her journey is a tapestry of achievements that span healthcare, finance, community outreach, artistry, and empowerment.

With an Associate Degree in Occupational Therapy, Dr. Kimberly's commitment to holistic well-being began early. Her passion for helping others thrive led her to earn a Bachelor's and Master's Degree in Health Administration, as well as a Doctorate in Humane Letters. As a Certified Holistic Health Coach & Certified Life Coach, Kimberly extends her expertise to guide individuals toward healthier lifestyles. Her holistic approach combines medical knowledge with a deep understanding of the mind-body connection, empowering her clients to achieve sustainable well-being.

Dr. Kimberly's influence extends to the financial realm, where she currently thrives as a Licensed Financial Professional. Specializing in optimizing wealth strategies, she helps families across the United States maximize their resources, save money, and minimize tax burdens, enabling them to secure their financial futures. Dr. Kimberly's commitment to financial empowerment is unwavering, as she extends her expertise and services to all, regardless of their financial status. She excels in guiding clients toward building a solid wealth trajectory and securing a comfortable retirement. Kimberly recognizes that the connection between financial security and health underscores the importance of holistic well-being.

Dr. Kimberly's voice reaches beyond the realm of finance and health. As a co-host of the K&O Show on WVOL (a historic African American radio station in Nashville, Tennessee), she utilizes the platform to provide insight, education, and inspiration to listeners while spotlighting community, healthcare, and faith-based leaders. Her commitment to community outreach is evident by her volunteering with Compassion International. She also forged partnerships with numerous organizations across Tennessee to organize a diverse array of charitable and community events. In her multifaceted journey of community service, Kimberly's former volunteer role as a sign language interpreter at Mt. Zion Church in Nashville and at various faith-based events featuring notable personalities like Barak Obama, Kirk Franklin, Fred Hammond, and Canton Jones stands as a testament to her unwavering dedication to promoting inclusion and unity.

Dr. Kimberly's compassion and dedication extend to her mission of creating positive change. Her visionary spirit shines as she is currently developing a non-profit agency dedicated to single mothers with children with special needs, inspired by her own personal journey with a granddaughter with special needs. Her past service on the boards of various non-profit organizations highlights her commitment to empowering and educating.

Dr. Kimberly is a devoted mother of three and grandmother of six. She enjoys traveling, ballroom dancing, attending concerts, movies, and shopping. She finds expression through her love for writing poetry and music. Her former role as a saxophonist and lyricist in Nashville showcased her spiritual connection and creative prowess. Presently, she continues to inspire and uplift, leaving an indelible mark on every facet of her journey.

CHAPTER FOUR
A JOURNEY OF BECOMING...
ANDREA HANCOCK

DEDICATION

This book is a heartfelt dedication to the cherished souls who have been the pillars of my existence. Above all, I offer my sincerest thanks to God, my unwavering companion who watched over and sustained me through every twist and turn. To all those who have walked alongside me on this tedious journey of becoming, each of your presence has been my greatest blessing.

A special tribute to Mary Davis, my beautiful grandmother, whose unwavering faith and prayers guided me.

To my mother, Norma Jean Hancock, my father, William Hancock, and my beloved sister, Angela Hancock- your legacy will forever live on in my heart.

Trixie Williams, a true friend and sister in every sense. Your unconditional love mirrored the divine.

I extend my deepest gratitude to my dear Mother and Pastor Harold J. Frelix Sr., whose wisdom and guidance have illuminated my path.

To my cousins Curtis and Shermica Hunt, you have truly been my anchors of support.

To my children James, Em'Maja, Jeanesia, DaSean, and Gregory, along with my grandchildren and extended family, your love has been my greatest reward. It has been the bedrock of my journey.

And to all women on their journey of becoming, may this chapter inspire and uplift you.

With heartfelt gratitude,

Andrea

A JOURNEY OF BECOMING...
ANDREA HANCOCK

*Disclaimer ** The story told below is the author's version of life events as they took place. The author recognizes that other people's memories of the events described in the book may differ from her own. The details are not intended to hurt, defame, or offend anyone.*

There have been times in my life when it was like playing a role in some old fictional "black exploitation" movie from my youth. Everyone's seen TV shows that have the scenes of the "late nights and early mornings" out in the streets. The people are out like zombies, thinking of no one but themselves and where the next "hit of satisfaction" will come from. However, the "pimps" don't always drive the fanciest cars and wear the outlandishly garish clothes, and the "hoes" are not that pretty and made up.

Still, like a scene out of a popular crime drama, this night had everything…

The wrecked vehicle, a path of destruction behind it that would be impossible for a sober individual to make (and one didn't!), the "shady" criminal quickly leaving the scene, and a badly bleeding body left behind mangled among the bushes in a ditch, flashing lights of the local emergency response vehicles, precariously parked to form a half-assed perimeter, and the faces of their various occupants inscrutable as they milled about. They had seen it all before.

In this instance, the response time was above average...Thank God. It was the time of night or early morning when you couldn't even drum up a decent crowd of gawkers to, if for no other reason, point, criticize, and complain.

Out riding around earlier....

I had been up for several days by this time. My mind was playing tricks on me. I could barely think or keep my eyes open. I knew I needed to go in. I knew it was just a matter of time before I slipped up and something bad would happen. I hadn't eaten anything the entire day and maybe just a bag of chips or two in the last couple of days. My stomach churned on nothing but my stomach acids. I was on a mission of destruction. Yet, I just needed one more.

Then, this car pulls up and stops. There was a friend of a guy I used to date who was in prison at the time. On the street, they called him "Catfish," and he was riding with another guy. He said, "Ride with us; I got something for you." I got in the car, and we were off riding around smoking crack. At some point, I began to feel that the guy who was driving was behaving strangely. At least, that's what my drug-addled mind was concluding.

They had been out all-day smoking crack, where one hit turned into another and another, as it always does. After the money ran out, "Catfish" began going into convenience stores to "jack" them. You know, walk in and walk straight out with cases of beer without paying. They knew who to sell it to for quick money. After this round was gone, they dropped me off and said they would return for me later.

When they dropped me off, something in my gut was telling me to go in, but I had got that taste; I was off to the races once again. I remember being out there, still waiting on cars, watching the car headlights. Part of street life sometimes is the loneliness and uncertainty of waiting for God knows what. There's a lot of that. Waiting for crack, my only friend, to show up with its other unwanted visitors becomes a way of life. So, I stood right there on that corner into the wee hours of the morning. After a while, I could barely stand any longer. My knees were nearly buckling. My mind and eyes were playing tricks on me. I was somewhat delirious, so I decided to go in.

Right when I turned to walk away, out of nowhere, those familiar headlights appeared; it was them. They had come back to get me. I immediately jumped in. Little did I know this ride would nearly cost me my life.

I instantly asked for a "hit," and the guy gave me nothing but a push. I was sitting in the back seat, getting that "push," and feeling like I was melting into the seat.

As we headed to our final destination, where the real party was to take place, the driver (I can't say for certain I ever knew his name) kept staring at me through the rearview mirror. I've had many men look at me, but I couldn't figure this one out. I know I was pretty high, but this was beginning to freak me out. He blew out this big cloud of smoke from his nose like a possessed dragon; the next thing I knew, he clinched the steering wheel, hit the accelerator, and steered the car straight towards the gas station, all the while still staring at me.

It felt like we were flying. I remember the big Shell sign quickly getting bigger and bigger as we got faster and faster. I felt like we would hit the gas pumps and blow up! Immediately I thought… I've got to get out of here, so I attempted to open the door. I recall the car going so fast that it was extremely difficult to swing the door open. It was as if the wind was pressing against it. My thoughts became disjointed then, and suddenly, I pushed that door open.

My world went black...

I remember coming to... I was on my back, looking up. I tried to get up, but I couldn't move. I then thought to myself, I've really messed up now. I knew I was badly hurt. Then my grandma's voice came to me. It was like she was speaking to me while I was lying there.

She said, "Grandbaby, just call on the name of the Lord."

And I remember lying there saying, "Jesus, please help me."

Immediately after that, it felt like it was raining or like raindrops were falling on my skin, but it was more like they were penetrating my skin. A supernatural calm came over me. Then everything went completely black again as I passed out.

While going in and out that night, somehow, I was able to give the number of a friend of the family, and they called her, saying they had an unidentified woman there in the hospital trauma unit. They didn't know if I would make it through the night. They said I was hurt very severely, so she called my cousin, and he came to see me. I was on a respirator with tubes coming from me, hooked up to several monitors, and almost unrecognizable. A sight my family was barely able to look upon.

Three days later, I woke up with a police officer in the room. The cop wanted to know if the guys pushed me out of the car. I said, "No, I jumped out because I thought we were going to blow up." I could barely talk. I was in excruciating pain, and I could not sit up.

A close friend's mother, who worked at the trauma unit at the hospital, said when I came in, I was in bad shape. When I jumped out of the car, I ruptured my spleen on impact and had an emergency splenectomy. I also had severe road rash, a shattered ankle, and a busted-up mouth. I was bloody all over. They had to do skin grafts to repair the severe road rash injuries over my body, stitch up my mouth, and do surgery on my ankle.

I remember my grandma saying that she was watching TV when the accident made the news. She said that she was praying for that person. She didn't know it was me until later. I know God was with me because that night, if the wreck had happened anywhere else or if someone had tried to move me, I probably would have died because my internal bleeding was so severe.

When I left the hospital, I was going to stay at my cousin's house, but then this guy, "Mr. Tim," took me in. He was a "trick" I had met right before all that happened. I didn't want to live with my cousin on the straight and narrow just yet, so I called "Mr. Tim." He agreed to let me live with him. Although he took care of me, I still hit the streets after about two months with that boot on my leg because my ankle was still healing.

Remember the "unidentified woman" in the trauma unit? The one the cops didn't even know. I definitely knew a lot about her. Or did I? When do we know ourselves best or even find out the most about ourselves?

Hopefully, unrecognizable from the person before you, that woman was me. I am Andrea Hancock, a woman of God, a mother, a nana, and a friend. I am a Summa Cum Laude graduate of Tennessee State University. I am both blessed and privileged to wear many hats from Minister to Transformational Coach. I founded Healing,

Empowerment, and Restoration (HER) Christian growth housing ministry, "A Woman's Journey" empowerment workshop, and Nana's Circle.

At any given time, you can find me preaching, advocating for Opioid overdose education and awareness, counseling young girls who are involved in the juvenile justice system or foster care, and encouraging mothers who are fighting to regain custody of their kids. I also facilitate empowerment workshops, speak at conferences, mentor women from all walks of life, and help feed and clothe the unhoused, impacting many lives by prescribing healing strategies to all.

These days, I work to maintain a strong bond with each of my children and enjoy making memories with my grandchildren. I understand you cannot truly make up for mistakes made in the past, however, I have been given the opportunity to be the mother that, at one time, was impossible to be. Like many other worthwhile things in my life, motherhood is something I work on constantly. The people closest to me are my greatest blessings.

The experiences I've had (and they run the gamut from tragic to the blessed) allow me to relate to the real stories of others. Each scar, each moment of darkness, paints a picture of resilience and strength that no piece of paper can capture. When you share this communication, you encourage and transform the lives of others. I've walked the tangled paths of bureaucracy and hardship, and now I open doors for others, guiding them with compassion born from my own struggles.

In a world that's quick to judge, I've learned a profound truth: No matter what you've been through or even going through in life, don't judge it because you don't know what it truly is. These words are etched deep within me, a lesson learned through the trials that have shaped my journey and who I am today.

Despite the doubters and the naysayers, I hold on to hope like a precious gem. I have been written off more than once, but I remain undeterred. With a faith that could move mountains, I plant seeds of love and compassion that allow rose gardens to grow from concrete.

I minister to people during their darkest days. I hope my voice carries the weight of empathy earned through my living. From the depths of my own pain, I've found a purpose—to inspire hope in the hopeless and be a guiding light for those lost in the darkness.

Somehow, cases that cause the most frustration have a way of finding me, and that is a great motivator for me. Pursuing these cases requires facing the raw realities of suicide, emotional trauma, and mental anguish. Gifted through my experiences and made through my adversities, I know that my past struggles have shaped me into a vessel of hope. Throughout, I hold steadfast to my faith. I know God is with me. I emerge, bloody but unbowed, knowing that my survival was a testament to a higher purpose.

This is who I am today. It has been a long road to get here, a journey fraught with disappointment, heartache, and adversity. A passage in which I have been able to find the proverbial "silver lining." I say this because my journey allows me to share personal experiences that inspire hope in those from divergent paths of life. By sharing my truth, I am blessed to encourage and empower individuals and walk along with them on their journey of becoming. As I share my story with you, I believe it is important to start from the beginning.

It just seems like the beginning was so long ago…

Most people only understand their childhood once they become adults. Age and experience give them the context to judge, and we can all get pretty judgmental. While much of what I've felt in my life might seem a bit idyllic to some, my descriptions come through many views and many eyes. They are the eyes of a child, a naïve girl, a "hopeless" addict, and a successful woman. It is a matter of perspective.

I was lucky enough to feel like I was one of those "Daddy's little girls" growing up. I was the epitome of the "good" girl. I didn't give my parents any issues. I grew up in what I understood was a "nice neighborhood." There was the feeling that our block was like family. We all looked out for each other.

I had the things that I needed, including a lot of the material things that others didn't have. I remember having brand new outfits with "fresh kicks" to match at the beginning of every school year. Although I was a little on the chubby side, my mother always made sure that I was still ahead of the other girls style-wise. I was "fresh" every day, but something was still missing…

My grandfather was a minister. Because of that, Christ has always been a big part of my life. His light has always been there, shining on me even when I was deep into the evils of the world and couldn't see it. Faith is the thread that has held my life together, and my love for The Lord began at an early age.

I made great grades through school and enjoyed playing outside with my friends when I had the chance, always remembering to be inside well before dark. I loved all holidays, especially Easter and Christmas. On Easter Sunday, my momma would press my hair and dress my sister and I up like dolls. I would have the puffy dress, white shoes with the ruffled socks, matching ribbons in my hair, and my favorite, a pure white sweater with pearl-like buttons. We would wake up to baskets full of candy. And I was a child who absolutely loved candy!

This was my childhood as I saw it. And I'm pretty sure this is the part of the story where you're thinking, "So far, so good."

Well…

I remember my father was drunk and passed out in an adjacent room at our place the evening my sister was shot and killed by her boyfriend.

My sister was everything to me, but I didn't know it at the time because she was my sister. You know, the girl who slept in the other bed or sometimes right there beside you. Like that well-worn cliché, I didn't know who she was until she wasn't. She meant a lot to my mother and father, too. So much so that I am certain the tragic events surrounding her death contributed to my parent's early decline and demise. I also feel that this event had such a far-reaching effect on my development that it set me on my journey down that slippery slope into the street life.

On the night of my sister's murder, I was at the living room table studying for a big French test the next day. Suddenly, I was being shuffled off to the side during the excitement and was unaware of the true gravity of the situation. I remember thinking I would have to miss French class and not take the test. The naiveté of youth! All I thought about was that I would have to miss the test and help my sister on crutches. That's the worst-case scenario I had formulated in my mind even as, unbeknownst to me, she lay dying from a gunshot wound to the leg in front of our apartment. The thought never occurred to me that I would never see her alive again. My somewhat "fairy tale life" was shattered. The little girl in me died.

My family was never the same after my sister's death. Four years later, my dad died. I was about to give birth to my first child. He was excited at the thought of having his first grandson. Often, he would talk about having my son hang out with him, musing about spending time with him and teaching him things. Perhaps he was looking forward to his first grandchild to reset his own life. Unfortunately for us, my father was hospitalized the day before my son came home. He never got to meet his grandson. That's something I often think about because he was so excited, and there's almost the feeling of having let him down. He would do anything for me or give me what I wanted.

While nothing could ever take my father's place, my son's birth brought me some measure of solace and certainly helped me cope with my father's death.

But it wasn't enough...

Four years after my father died, I was in full-blown addiction and pregnant with my third child when my mother passed. I remember I was caring for my mama when she was in hospice care before she passed away. I recall her slipping down in the hospital bed while I was there. I was trying to grab her by her arms and pull her back up in the bed. I remember her faintly saying, "No, no," to which I replied, "No, Mom, it's OK." I asked her, "What's wrong?" and she said with a whisper… "You're pregnant." Even in my mama's weakness, she was still trying to take care of me.

When my "troubles" were going on, my mother never confronted me or asked me what was going on. I don't think she was willing to take a chance on losing another daughter by pushing me away. She loved me the best way that she knew how.

Sometimes, when you think you've hit the bottom, you still have a ways to go.

My first child's father was physically abusive to the point where he thought domestic violence was a solution, not a problem. When I met my second child's father, in my ignorance, I viewed him as my "knight in shining armor," the man who would rescue me from all the world's problems. I thought I had found something better. I thought I had found something different. In retrospect, what it really came down to was the "same ole…same ole."

When I think about my second child's father, my image of him was one of a "bad boy." You know, the kind we girls like that will "break the rules" we want broken and will say that they're "doing it all for you." He had the fancy car, glittery jewelry, nice clothes, and the charisma that sealed the deal. He was respected and feared in the "hood," and lived a flamboyant lifestyle I was not accustomed to. I looked at him as someone who could protect me from further hurt or harm.

He had a friend who always seemed to be around him, and I used to hang out with them. We would ride around, and I would watch while they smoked, but I wasn't into doing drugs or anything at the time. I tried marijuana maybe a time or two, but I didn't like the way it made me feel. I remember being with them, and they would smoke something I thought was marijuana because it would be rolled up in papers. I noticed that my child's father would only smoke around this guy, him, and no one else. I was always curious about what they were smoking. They were very secretive about what they were doing, and he would become upset when I would ask to take a hit from the joint. In retrospect, I suppose he was really looking out for me.

When you think you're in love…

Finally, after bugging him on one occasion, he said, "OK, Andrea, here you go. Buckle your seatbelt because you're getting ready to take a ride!"

He handed me the joint and told me to "take it easy." As I took a pull and inhaled the smoke, I remember immediately becoming sick to my stomach, and I started vomiting! I was feeling terrible, and I told him that I needed to go to the hospital because it felt like death was coming (like I'd know.) He told me I couldn't go to the hospital. When I asked why not, he said that there was cocaine in the joint.

I was shocked. Then I thought, "Oh my God, this is something bad, and he's given it to me."

After I got through that night, I continued to hang out with the fellows. I eased myself into smoking regularly, and eventually, I didn't get sick. The high and the rush that it gave me was "heavenly." It was explained to me that it was tobacco laced with crack cocaine crushed down in it. He would call this a "Primo." He said, "You don't want to smoke this without me because if you do, you'll end up a "junkie or clucker." Cocaine was always around and available to me. It was cool, or at least I thought.

I was in school at the time, a senior in my final semester, and an honor student to boot! He would come to pick me up from school, and my classmates would go crazy with excitement when he would pull up.

For the first time, I was getting all of this attention from my peers, and it felt great! It was also the first time I felt like I was popular. I was that girl with the handsome, popular, and intimidating "bad boy" with money. So, for me, this was huge.

It got to the point where I wanted to hang out with him more than anything else. I eventually dropped out in the last semester of my final year of high school. Talk about an omen of bad things to come! I was nominated among "Who's Who of America" for academic excellence, and I was supposed to be preparing for graduation. However, I got into this unhealthy relationship, started smoking crack cocaine, and just stopped going to school. This wasn't going to work…

My life intersected between becoming an adult and a drug addict. Of course, I had no idea the profound effect my choices would have on my life down the road. It was a voyage to become who I am today by being reduced to nothing before I could become something. In fact, it would be years before I finally embraced "The Unchanging Hand" and allowed God's help to come in.

The full narrative of my campaign to victory is a story for another time. I know this already sounds like a lot, but trust me, there is much more to my journey of becoming. I hope that by sharing this portion of my story, you will be encouraged, empowered, and inspired.

Just know God will take all of your disappointments and give you beauty for your ashes. Your purpose can be directly tied to your pain, and know that there is power in your pain. Going through trials and trouble gives you a different type of strength once you make it through. Trust the process but more importantly…Trust God.

ABOUT THE AUTHOR – ANDREA HANCOCK

Andrea Hancock's life is a testament to the profound nature of transformation, a journey that unfolds from a seed-like existence with the potential to blossom into something extraordinary. Her early years were marked by the fulfillment of basic needs and academic excellence, portraying her as an honor student and generally a happy child. However, these promising elements were interspersed with the weeds of trauma, the loss of family members, unhealthy relationships, substance abuse, involvement in crime, and work in the sex industry—adverse experiences that would challenge even the strongest individuals.

Once imprisoned by drugs and alcohol, Andrea was released in 2006 by the power of God and restored to her rightful role as a mother and productive member of society. Andrea Hancock's metamorphosis is a remarkable model of hope for women overcoming diverse obstacles.

Andrea accepted the LORD's call on May 21, 2006, and became a licensed Minister on October 9, 2011, and an ordained Elder on November 16, 2014. Who would have dreamed that Andrea would emerge to epitomize hope, change, restoration, resilience, and empowerment for thousands of women?

Led by divine inspiration, Elder Hancock founded A Woman's Journey, Healing, Empowerment and Restoration (HER) Christian Growth Housing Ministry and, most recently, Nana's Circle, a community that supports aging caregivers. Andrea graduated with honorary excellence, Summa Cum Laude from Tennessee State University, with a Bachelor of Science degree in Social Work. She is a statewide Licensed Alcohol and Drug Abuse Counselor

(LADAC II), Certified Peer Recovery Specialist (CPRS), and Certified Anger Management Specialist (CAMS I).

Andrea was recognized and honored at Natalie Grant's event "Dare to Be" for her work with feeding young adults in Downtown Nashville. Andrea was featured in the 2018 Good Grit magazine for her work with Epic Girl, working with at-risk youth. In 2023, Andrea received the Humana Hometown Heroes Award for community dedication and service, presented by MDHA's Resident Association. Andrea is a highly sought-after guest speaker for both faith-based and community programs. Andrea covers diverse topics seeking to provide education, inspiration, and hope to women from all walks of life. Andrea will soon be noted for her work as an author of her book titled "She Didn't Know: A Woman's Journey of Becoming."

Andrea would like to be known as a woman who has emerged from her traumatic and paralyzing past experiences and continues to grow as a woman of faith, presenting and prescribing healing strategies for others. Andrea embraces her ongoing work of self-love and forgiveness, driven by the reward of being an inspiration and spending quality time with her family while maintaining unshakeable faith. Andrea praises God for her imperfect yet continual journey of becoming.

CHAPTER FIVE
DESTINATION SUCCESS
DUANECHEL HARRIS

DEDICATION

As the days wind down, getting closer to the deadline made me realize how grateful I am to those who walked this journey before me.

Cleaving to the very things that they taught me to sustain, not always meeting the mark but forever standing, I pay homage to my grandmothers Effie Brown, Ellie Harris, Effie Coger, Annie Lou Harris, and Kim Johnson, a dear friend.

Not forgetting the male figures who played a part in my life, thank you:

William Harris

Alfred Hilton

Kent Melbourne

Bishop Leslie Grace, Interdenominational New Vision Church

Bishop Orr Rock, United Ministries

And to those Superheroes for literally showing me that nothing worth having is easily obtained.

My mother, Jayma Melbourne

Carolyn Jennings

Stacy Bryant

Camilla Jones

Peaches

Anna Campbell

Pastor Janet Ridley, my personal songstress

Angela Blakely

Clemmie Greenlee/Community Activist and Leader

To my children, I thank you for picking me to be your mom, and I hope this shows you that nothing is impossible, no matter how hard it may seem.

I want to give a special thanks to the late Beverly Kindall and Ms. Quick, my honors English teachers, who gave me my first opportunity to be published.

L.M. Collins, English Professor Emeritus/

Fisk University

Markesha C./My Bus Driver

Born to Write the Poet

Don Polk, I thank you for your love and encouragement when I felt I had no words to write.

Most of all, I dedicate this chapter to me for having the ability and support to remove the bandages and to heal the wounds.

For I Will Not Give Up On Me!

Destination Success, Here I Come!

DESTINATION SUCCESS

DUANECHEL HARRIS

Close your eyes and open your hearts, for on this road, we will travel down through the Mississippi cotton fields to the old Tennessee hills to the other side of Highway 269.

Riding in a Baby Blue Caddy, baby shining like new money.

To a small valley where I was conceived, for you know, it says lilies are made in the valley.

They can bloom into the winter months and survive if given the proper care.

See, Lilly OValley is my name.

So, all winter long, I was kept under lock and key.

Then, one day, I was set out for display.

It was time for me to serve my purpose, bringing joy, peace, and a smile to someone's day.

Perky, standing up straight, vibrant in color, ready to bloom.

When I suddenly started to lean to the right, then a little to the left, confused on every hand on which way to go, just wanting to be the chosen one.

I set out for my quest which was the other side.

Traveling to the Other Side

It's hot; the sun is beaming.

See the young woman as she's walking down the street.

People everywhere; her dress is flowing back and forth, side to side, as her hips glide.

Not even a cool breeze to help her catch her breath.

Oh, was she tied! (teen pregnancy, molestation, fatherlessness, death, high school dropout)

Did u say tied? (single parent, drug addiction, domestic violence, overcoming statistics for racial barriers, women's entrepreneurship, being a leading lady)

Oh yes, I did say tied.

Why you say she tied?

Cause old man Jellie would say she been…

road like a roller coaster…

an old dish rag…

wet and hung up to dry…

Ooooooo well, hold on… child, let me tell ya!

She was brought here to these hills from the cotton fields

where they sang the old negro spirituals that helped them to push on.

She was made to believe she was some kind of pretty

Falling in and out of circumstances to build up only to be torn down.

Remember I told you it was hot outside, for her inner peace had been shaken.

As she pressed on, there were people showing love everywhere,

but it was like a long, cold winter night.

Alone while standing in the crowd, she began to cross to the other side.

So, she moved through the crowd, trembling, as her palms became sweaty.

Her heart beating like the panting of a dog in need of water.

Intensely greeting those with whom her eyes connected,

finally making it to the other side.

She understood that the oppression became suppression

with some discretion caused depression.

No sleep, couldn't eat.

Her wheels were forever spinning.

The mind of a movie screen: Images of what was and what was to come.

Child, but I tell you one thing for sho,' she never let go!

She told me 'bout the night she cried out.

How something strange overcame her and saved her from her.

Believe me, she knew what that something strange was.

It was the hand of the Most High with His Great Mighty Power

just breathing on her, giving her that breath she needed to carry on.

Then there was the time when she felt like giving up, and something lifted her up.

All while wailing, she was winning, not quite understanding at the time,

but she knew she had to get to the other side.

See, the key was getting to the other side. It was a setup.

For I tell you, she had to wail to win.

You can now open your eyes to see me cause she has been me.

So, I wail on this day.

For I boast not of the things of myself,

but of things in which my Father in heaven is doing in me.

So every day I win!

So let me tell you…

Humpty Dumpty fell off the wall; Humpty Dumpty had a Great FALL.

It is said that all the King's horses and all the King's men

couldn't put Humpty back together again.

Let me just tell you why!

For it was me, I was Humpty.

I fell off the wall so many times I can't remember them all.

Disobedience…

Teen Pregnancy…

Bad relationships… one after another, whether it was men or family.

Drugs…

Systematic oppression which causes depression.

A lab rat in a cage spinning its wheels like a gerbil.

One sho' got tired of the wheels spinning. And it was time for it to stop at once!

Understanding that nothing happens overnight, it was time to find a new direction

for the purpose of the mission, which is to live.

Stand no matter how hard the wind blows.

Be like that tree planted by the riverside that shall not be moved,

for its roots will hold it down.

Being broken into so many pieces, some big… some small,

I had to address the elephant in the room. He had been there since birth.

This aided me in writing the chapter called "Separation" in *Broken Crayons Still Color 2*.

Addressing that trauma allowed me to acknowledge my scars

and begin to heal wounds that no man could heal, for it was a "Me" disease.

I had allowed the infestation of things in my life to manipulate my entire makeup.

My habits changed my habitation; the vessel was off course.

The intake was giving questionable output, the quality control was not at its best.

All innocence and purity were gone, for the choices which had been made

were detrimental to my being.

There was love, money, knowledge, wise counsel, and resources as far as I could reach

but it was just not enough while in that space.

I literally had to separate myself.

Fighting Her Way Back

While yet determined to make it to the other side,

Determined to do a lot while fighting to live.

The cherry ball has been released.

It exploded… shit hit the floor and went everywhere

causing all types of dysfunctional fluctuations.

Communication grid was a complete loss,

while it was no longer about the relationship with man,

it was the relationship with self.

When she neglected and lost herself,

she lost her connection to the very thing that allowed her to be.

It shut her inner connection to the God within, making her soul grieve.

Taking vexation, that caused her pride to swallow her whole,

Disrupting the metabolic structure in which she was designed.

So, I went about gathering all my pieces; I told you there were a lot of pieces.

Solitude, here I come.

****

I closed myself off from the very things I loved, my family, friends, and social interactions, while still loving and serving them. I began to collect the things needed to put me back together; I just wanted to be whole again. I got my sword, a dictionary, a few books by my favorite author, Iyanla Vanzant, a pin and paper, and invested in some coaching sessions.

I did a little networking with a few of my most trusted associates, who understood my need to participate and my position in my absence. They assisted in giving me the opportunity to serve in my solitude. I began connecting to the very thing that allowed me to sustain, which was the Most High God and Mother Earth, overstanding to understand that her womb is where I reside.

For me to continue, I must serve with all that I have in me, for we all, each living thing that was created and placed here on this planet, have a job to fulfill within this life cycle. That is why it is called a life cycle. We were put here to serve one another with our greatest abilities. For that task, I realized I had to get a grip on things to meet the mark of the high calling.

With the many gifts bestowed upon my hands, a daily opportunity that was once taken for granted—the ability to speak and the possession of a Mighty POWER of love and strength—I put my big girl drawers on, as my mother would call them, and went to work. For it had already been written the road that I must travel, and it was high time for the cord to be cut—no more addictions, no more crutches, no more disrespect from anyone for that matter. The lonely nights that had been filled with tears from the empty nest syndrome and infidelity have now turned into moments of desire. It was like a resuscitation was being performed in an emergency room.

My inner parts started to gain life with every waking moment that I focused on myself. I took time to see me, the woman in the mirror. I checked off the things I liked, those I did not, and how I could fix them by listing all the things from such a gifted skill set. I began to get up each day, being thankful for another chance at getting it right, making sure I did not look how I felt. Believe me, it was not always an easy job.

I began reaching out to my support system; I created my own tribe, a group of individuals I trusted, that would help me to see and add value to myself and also hold me accountable for things in which we came into agreement about with regards to whom I had been called to be. Plans for financial stability were given. I never imagined I would have income due to the lack of knowledge I later gained while making corrections to my process. Seedlings started to pop everywhere. I did not know which way to go, so I began addressing those things that gave me my most joyous moments, which were helping others heal while I was in the process of healing myself with herbal treatments, meditation on the word, and calling all of my power back to me.

This regimen got my blood flowing, my heart pumping, and a genuine smile. I no longer entered the room with a lack of confidence, but I entered the room with all eyes on me as if I had never been seen before. I could feel the wounds repairing themselves. Taking it step by step, and second after second, I managed to gain enough strength to stand, even in the moments of despair when the pain was unbearable, and I felt as if my heart would not beat again. I reached back for those things which gave me joy. I knew the many possibilities it could present, and the ability to accomplish them was more than enough to try again and again.

In that space that I occupied, there were all kinds of gadgets made for me to use to hold my balance. The gadgets were removed as the wounds held together, and the pieces began to slowly fuse themselves back together like a fractured fibula encased to heal. The diagnoses had been given, and the prescription had been written. I was advised to seek more knowledge.

I bought books and herbs and made healthier choices for the things I ingested. I also had social interactions with others who were either headed to my same destination or had been there for a while. I was advised that this would clear the mind so that the body would fall in line and heed its command.

Taking a stand for what I believe and what I know to be right according to the laws of the land, I moved in such a way that one would be an imposter. Seeing that when I changed my stance, it changed my direction, giving me a new perspective and a different outlook, allowing me to see life through a different lens; I activated the renewing of my mind. What was once a dark place became a light on my path.

With the remembrance of my Great-Great-Grandmother repeating the Serenity Prayer, my position changed from bent over and fatigued to upright like the Statue of Liberty holding her torch, lighting the way to freedom—a Freedom that no man can give. Inner peace, unspeakable joy, confidence, and a desire to strive and make it to the mountaintop were the guiding forces to get me to the other side, leading me to my destination called Success.

I had the power to change the things that involved me, except for those things that I could not. I set out to be the best version of myself that I could be. Understanding the difference between a want and a need may seem futile, but believe me, it can also be a hindrance. Indeed, a readjustment was needed in order to accomplish the other goals that would have a dramatic effect on my change.

Only then was I able to say no more to trying to defend myself in pointless situations that would not bring life nor death, put food on my table or any money in my pocket, nor the continual efforts of finding validation from others or the need to feel loved. Even looking for someone to make me happy was no longer an issue. And I will tell you why, because now when deciding to be a mother, a wife, a servant, or an entrepreneur, I was no longer Duanechel Harris, who had taken an oath of commitment. I became that Lilly in the Valley, for I had to know that I could weather the storm no matter what came my way, trusting, even sometimes doubting, my ability at times to complete the task. I had to lean on the things I had acquired to make it through, like meditating on the word and serving even when I felt down and out.

Even when I felt I was not worthy of the task, I had to fight. I had to be bold and confident, for the race is not given to the swift but to the one who endures. So, you see, doubting made it harder than it was because I had allowed myself to be removed from my original place of habitation all due to a desire. I experienced brick wall after brick wall, dead ends, caution signs, and, of course, some detours as I tried to reroute the vessel, but it was about empty. I could not stand it anymore; I was withering away.

The water was filled with chemicals that drowned my roots, and the ground was tainted with bad fertilizer. I had lost my identity. I thought I was a weed instead of a beautiful Peace

Lily. I kept having to do a triple-take to see if that was really what I was seeing. One moment, I wanted to die or thought it was over, and from nowhere, there came a light shining bright.

Finally, one day, someone came by and dug me up by my roots from the valley, took me, and planted me in some new dirt, giving me hope and a future. I was able to identify myself with the information that had been given about who I was and how I would stand according to who I was called to be.

The process took about three years of picking and prodding, digging my roots a little deeper to get to the root of the issue, which was getting me to the point of writing the vision and making it visible in plain sight. I needed that to activate the Power. I needed to see the seedling produce the blossom. I was told it would produce it because lilies can die off, but they will bloom again if given the proper protection from the elements of the air. This allows them to process clusters of other lilies by germination from the black spots on them, which are actually called aerial bulbs. They fall to the ground, producing more and more and more lilies, populating the world in which they live with a place of peace seen by the eye as a beautiful flower, one of the most desired to bring blessings to many.

So, after being pruned and nurtured back to what was known to be natural to me, taking root in what I know as Lily, which would be good soil and fertilizer in the carnal, I had to reconnect to the very being of my existence and begin to repair the wounds and afflictions of my way so that I would be able transition into the Power of knowing who I am and the only thing that could stop me was me.

I begin repeating the Serenity Prayer over and over to myself, telling myself that I must be like the tree planted by the riverside that can't be moved—stand no matter what!

So, when times get overwhelming and out of control, I dig my roots a little deeper so that I may withstand the test, for my reward is success.

All aboard the vessel, landing at a destination called Success.

Space
Inches
Centimeters
Seconds, hours, days which turn into weeks, and then months into years of unspoken pains
Calibrations are calculated by the very breath that you breathe.
Feeling the intensity of the blood flowing to your heart
Confused but yet boldly do you stand
Questionable is your success
While the cup is half full, although it still seems as empty as it can be, nothing is there.

Dry
Guided by such a mighty force.

Wind blowing
You bend, but You never break.
Structure cultivates identity.

Success is the rebirth of the most beautiful thing I have ever seen. A flower that had been drowned from the roots to the point of what I felt was mold, a fungus that had grown to take over my roots. No one would find me; the mask of the imposter would not come off. The spots on me were from the exposure to the bad elements of my habitation. There was no germination or pollination of any sort.

Suddenly, I could hear it from afar. A stream of water flowed, rushing from the rocks. It seemed as if it was very close, getting closer and closer to me, for I was fatigued from the explosion, the overload of life, and its circumstances. The sound of the water got closer to me, not knowing that the harder I dug my roots into the surface I was creating a means for the very thing that would help me to sustain life to have access again. I felt a trickle to my toes; they began to wiggle from being stuck in the same position for so long. You know, it's called stagnation.

Suddenly, my leaves began to move, and my eyes began to open. The bloom was opening, and all I could see were places where I had left my mark, smiles, joy, and people fulfilling their lifelong dreams. Call centers giving people the ability to enjoy life with the flexibility needed to spend that quality time with loved ones or even just to take a moment to smell the lilies for the sweet aroma they produce. Vessels being cleaned and reset, getting ready for takeoff to their desired destination. Bystanders wowing in amazement at the thought of them seeing the plucking of my roots, believing it would be the last they saw or heard from me.

The reassurance that you can and will live serves your intended purpose for this life: to bring knowledge, love, joy, and peace, an energy that will stretch beyond as far as the eyes can see. The energy is so exhilarating that as it travels the skies, making its way through the galaxy, it sprinkles a little bit of itself here and there, creating a massive power, a call for freedom, a freedom that will not be televised, just felt from within. For remember, it says in his word, a tree is known by the fruit which it bears. Paraphrasing, but you get my point.

Life was restored by the most natural source of all, the water from the womb of the mother. I'm being made whole. I can swim the banks of the Jordan, for the tide has been lowered for me to pass by. But while I am here, it is my birthright to stand as a free human being in my power and not be ashamed of who I am and what I choose to believe in, whether it be pleasing to others or not, but serving with a moralistic compass that will direct my path as I conquer the bumps in the road to make it to destination success.

So, you see, it was a curse devised by the enemy who made me believe that I was not called to greatness, to have over and beyond my imagination, see places, and create life-lasting relationships, creating avenues for people and women who desire to be free from within.

For today, I stand before you with my pin scratching out and highlighting some of my better moments while trying to decide which squiggly line to erase some of my written mistakes and correcting my literary pin. Take a walk with me as we embark upon the freedom train. The journey may be long, but the track has been cleared.

You will need to pack your lunch because there will be small breaks but continuous work for hours and days ahead. You will get there without a shadow of a doubt, for you must trust the process, knowing that nothing worth having will ever come easy. You control your destination, and it is all up to you.

ABOUT THE AUTHOR - DUANECHEL HARRIS

Duanechel Harris, a native of Nashville, Tennessee, is known as Lilly OValley in the Poetic community. She is the founder and CEO of M.V.P. Consulting Corporation and Vonpias Herbal Treatments, where a variety of services are offered at both professional and holistic levels.

She focuses on and takes pride in helping individuals heal the whole Soul. Through her studies, she understands that the only way to completely heal the body is to heal the mind, and then the body will fall into line.

Duanechel's education and time spent serving the people under the direction of Bishop Timothy Q. Leslie and Bishop Samuel Orr, along with the Walking in Purpose Organization, a non-profit organization that was founded, allowed her to collaborate on several different community activities. She established her very own Annual Backpack Giveaway with the help and support of a few Black-owned businesses within the community.

Vonpias Herbal Treatments was established from some long nights of study due to being diagnosed with Hypothyroidism and having an aunt who is a Diabetic Amputee. Duanechel then developed Killer Pain Cream. During the COVID-19 Pandemic, she produced Elderberry Tinctures, which have been recommended as an Immune Booster. It has been in stock at ALKE BA LAN Images for two years.

Duanechel helps individuals make healthier decisions for a better life through her business and personal development coaching. She is an Evangelist, Certified Life Coach, Yoni Steam Practitioner, and a Certified Community Health Care worker. In addition, she is the owner-operator of At Home Call Center and A Cleaning Service. She also holds the title of a published Poet and An International Best-Selling Author. She takes pride in knowing that she can be a part of not just her own healing but that of others as well. It sparks a fire inside for the wheels to keep turning.

M.V.P. Consulting Corporation is to be the catalyst for change in facilitating management. Leveraging her unique skill set and complement to community well-being, she will create a tailored solution that drives success for her clients and positively impact the world around them.

CHAPTER SIX
MY WINGS ARE FINALLY READY
Dr. Patricia Jackson

ACKNOWLEDGMENTS

To my Divine Love God, Yahweh, Holy Spirit, thank you for life, unconditional love, mercy, guidance, and that gentle nudge to make the decision to venture out of my comfort zone to write this chapter. I thank you!

To Dr. Tanya Davis for being the visionary that you are in presenting this opportunity of a lifetime, and Angela Lewis for your expertise and skills in putting everything together. I thank you!

To Mama, Daddy, my grandma Mi-Mama, and my honey Amos, I know you are so proud of me, and I feel your love and support from the heavens.

To my children, Vonnie, Jack, Venessa, Tsan, and EJ, you all are my biggest fans and cheerleaders. I love you all to the moon and back, and I thank you for the gifts and blessings that you are and for insisting that there is no option for me not to live my better than best life.

To my only sibling, my sister Pamela Streator Dixson, it was just the two of us, and I thank you for your love and support. I am just as proud of you for being the awesome woman that you are.

To my sister/cousin Thea Copeland, you have always had my back, and I thank you.

To my pastor and first lady, Dr. James and Dr. Inger Dunn, I thank you for your love, leadership, and ministry, which have contributed to and assisted in my spiritual growth and fulfillment of my purpose.

To my aunt, Helen Streator Hill, I know you have always loved me and supported me. I thank you and honor you as you are about to celebrate your 90th birthday.

To my dear friends and traveling companions, the Huffs and the Raineys, I cherish our friendship, fun trips, and future journeys. I thank you all for being the rocks I could lean on during a very hard time and for your love and support.

There are many more family members, friends, and others who have been and continue to be such an integral part of my life. I thank you and appreciate you from the depths of my heart and soul for the many ways you have contributed to my life and in whatever capacity.

MY WINGS ARE FINALLY READY
DR. PATRICIA JACKSON

Disclaimer ** The story told below is the author's version of life events as they took place. The author recognizes that other people's memories of the events described in the book may differ from her own. The details are not intended to hurt, defame, or offend anyone.

Where do I start? Where do I begin? Imagine being 71 years old and going through a metamorphosis you thought you had already experienced. The butterfly had emerged, only to learn that the process had not been completed at all until now. WOW! And although I had already emerged and taken flight, it was only so high and definitely not to the level that God had intended for me to fly. Perhaps it's even been like the process that birds go through when they are molting (shedding old feathers to make way for new ones.) Whatever process it has been, it is definitely a process of re-creation, and as a result, it now resonates more with me why my grief counselor stated that I was recreating myself. You are probably wondering why this is. Well, allow me to take you on a little journey.

I am the oldest of two children. My sister and I grew up in a two-parent household, where Mama was a great stay-at-home mom, and Dad was the provider. My Dad was a fast learner and a very smart man. I felt like there was nothing he could not do. As I got older, I realized how much of a perfectionist he was. I adored my dad; however, growing up with him had its difficult moments. Because he was such a fast learner, he was very impatient with me when I did not learn or comprehend something quickly.

One particular incident was when I was learning to spell my name. I couldn't quite get the letters right, so he raised his voice. He could not understand why I was not getting it, and I got a smack on the hand. This, along with other occurrences, led to the beginning of my journey to having feelings of inadequacy and becoming a people pleaser and conflict avoider.

My mama always told me what a pleasant, even-tempered child I was and not one to give any problems, yet instead of developing my voice and my identity, I lost mine. In later years, my dad and I were able to discuss this. He apologized and was genuinely sorry. I learned that his own issues shaped his behavior, and he did not realize the consequences of his actions. However, it shaped and affected my life for many years.

Fast forward to 15-year-old me, who met a boy in my biology class who became my high school sweetheart and my first for everything. I was so very naive. We became teenage parents of a beautiful baby girl at the age of 17, and that was the beginning of a journey that would take me to a very dark place. He was insecure and controlling, but of course, I did not see that at first, even though I got my first slap when I was 16 because he thought I was talking to another boy. We got married at the age of 19 after he had a baby with another young lady, and I broke up with him but took him back. Am I confusing you yet?

We were married for nine years, and during that time with him, I moved to Florida, added three more children, had financial success, financial loss, evictions, homelessness, and experienced physical, emotional, financial, and spiritual abuse as well as spousal rape. Add to that the drug usage and abuse issues that he had. It was only through the grace and strength of God that I escaped the grasp of drug addiction.

My children and I would be left at home, barely surviving for days at a time, sometimes without electricity or water, while their father went to cheat and hang out. We would have no money or food, leaving me to borrow from my neighbors, or my parents would miraculously send money at just the right time.

Why did I stay? That was my husband, and you don't leave your husband. At least that's what I thought. When you get married, it's for life. A woman on a prayer line told me I needed to pray, and I did. I went to church with my children, and when we returned home, I was beaten and accused of dating the men in the congregation. However, I did not stop going. I wore the same dress every Sunday and always held onto my faith.

My pastor became aware of what was going on in my life through a very precious friend of mine. He had a caring conversation with me and stated, "Daughter, God does not mean for a marriage to be like this." That was what it took to start the wheel turning and even entertain the fact of leaving. Because I had become a people pleaser due to the trauma I experienced with my biological Dad, I felt like I would not be pleasing my heavenly Father if I ended my marriage.

Eventually, it became clear that my safety was more in jeopardy than ever, so I made the decision to leave. This resulted in a plan of escape for me and my children to a domestic violence shelter. Thankfully, we were there for only a weekend, as my parents arranged for us to travel back home to Nashville.

It would probably be presumptuous to think this was the end of my journey, but it wasn't. My children and I moved in with my parents; however, their father found out we were back home and came trying to woo me back. I almost gave in to his pleas like usual, but not this time. This time, it became a fight for my survival that nearly resulted in me taking his life.

So, what happened from there? Well, I picked myself up, brushed myself off, got a divorce, and knew I had to move full steam ahead to take care of my family. However, little did I know how deeply wounded and damaged I was. I thought I was doing well in my life, and to a certain extent, I was. I got a good job through a friend's recommendation, then applied to LPN school and got accepted.

It wasn't until I started dating again that the effects of the abuse I endured began to surface from the depths of my core. There were so many changes I went through. I had trust issues, rejection issues, and very low self-esteem and self-worth, on top of dealing with anxiety and depression, almost becoming anorexic, and being a total emotional wreck. In fact, I nearly had a mental breakdown. That is what pushed me to begin counseling for the very first time. This was the beginning of my healing journey, but it would be a continuous process.

Over the years, many life events, accomplishments, joyous occasions, and heartaches have occurred. I furthered my education and received my associate degree in nursing to become an RN, which led to a 32-year medical career. I was in a marriage again for 26 years that ended in divorce, (that's another story in itself for another day) while raising my children with all the events that transpired with that ordeal. I also became a grandmother, started a new profession after going back to school again to receive my Ph.D. as a Licensed Clinical Pastoral Counselor, became the caregiver for both of my parents, started dating my ex-husband again, and had many more counseling and therapy sessions leading to more healing.

My parents passed away within five months of each other in 2021, and my ex-husband/friend, yes, my love, died suddenly and unexpectedly in November of 2022. These losses broke my heart, and the grief has been devastating and has me now in grief counseling. My family, friends, and others often tell me I am a strong woman. However, I tell them God's power, grace, love, and strength have sustained me.

I have been very determined to embrace change and leave myself open for whatever God would have me to do. Has it been easy? I have to say hell no! Sometimes, the pain was so intense that it literally took my breath away. Psalm 34:18 says, *"The Lord is near to the brokenhearted and saves the crushed in spirit."* I have held Him to His word so very many times.

Most women my age are probably what we might refer to as "settled" in life by this time, which can be referred to as the latter years and chapter of life. NOT ME!! I feel I am really just beginning to live and not just survive. That's where the re-creation I mentioned at the beginning of this chapter comes into play. Man, I just became a first-time homeowner at the age of 70! I am now living alone after having others with me since I was 17.

Have I been at rock bottom? Yes, I have! Have I been going through a metamorphosis or molting? Yes, I have! I can now say that I might be able to relate to how the caterpillars and birds feel as they undergo their transformation. Ouch!

In 2023, I said it was the year to be free, although I did not fully realize what that meant. I've struggled and fought for my freedom for many years. A fight to free myself from being a people pleaser and conflict avoider, a fight to heal from trauma and feelings of inadequacy, a fight to build my self-esteem and self-worth, and a fight to find my voice and identity. I've been under construction, and now my wings are finally ready. In 2024, this rock star is ready to soar to the highest of heights!

What will this look like for me? Ultimately, I will be an open canvas and vessel for God to use me in whatever capacity is needed and He sees fit. I will continue counseling and assisting others in their mental, emotional, and spiritual healing as they transform into their healthy, higher selves. I hope to be an example to others, especially women, that age is just a number, and your life isn't over because you reach your "senior" years, and you don't have to settle because you have more years behind you than before you. Life is meant to be lived, and I plan to do just that!

There are and will continue to be plans for travel to places on my bucket list and great experiences with family and friends. And you know, sometimes there will be times of doing nothing, just relaxing with no agenda, reading a good book, or watching movies all day. I definitely will make sure I stay as physically healthy as possible with exercise, nice leisurely walks, and healthy eating. Still, I will not deprive myself of tasting the delicacies of life either. It will definitely be quite a flight. I'm ready!!

ABOUT THE AUTHOR – DR. PATRICIA JACKSON

Dr. Patricia Streator Jackson, PhD is a certified licensed pastoral counselor. She is lovingly known as Dr. Mom to her children and Dr. Pat or Dr. J by her friends and clients. Her purpose and passion are to help guide and empower others to become mentally and emotionally healthy and to assist them in meeting themselves often for the very first time. As a domestic abuse survivor, she knows how vital this is. Dr. Pat knows change is hard, and staying the same is hard. However, you must choose your hard and choose to change.

Dr. Pat is also a retired cardiac registered nurse, senior associate pastor at Purpose International Life Changing Ministries, an academic instructor at the Institute of Counselor Development, board member of Women Who Rock Nashville, where she serves as mental health therapist for the board, and a motivational and transformational speaker and teacher.

Her academic achievements include graduate of the Institute of Counselor Development, where she received her Bachelor's, Master's, and Ph.D. in Christian counseling, an associate degree in Nursing from Tennessee State University, and a Pearl Senior High School graduate.

She is a certified Temperament Counselor, a Professional member of the Sarasota Academy of Christian Counseling, and a Professional and Pastoral Member of the National Christian Counselor Association. She has Advanced Certification in Crisis and Abuse Therapy.

Dr. Pat is a mom and grandmother and loves spending time with her family. In her leisure time, she listens to music (loves smooth jazz), volunteers with WFSK 88.1 jazz radio station, loves reading and watching good movies, and travels every chance she gets.

CHAPTER SEVEN
BELIEVING IN NEW BEGINNINGS
CHRISTINA KELLY

DEDICATION

To my wonderful and Almighty GOD, who has inspired me, and to my husband and two boys, who keep me going.

BELIEVING IN NEW BEGINNINGS

CHRISTINA KELLY

"Therefore, if anyone is in Christ, he is a new creation; old things have passed away; behold, all things have become new." 2 Corinthians 5:17

*Disclaimer ** The story told below is the author's version of life events as they took place. The author recognizes that other people's memories of the events described in the book may differ from her own. The details are not intended to hurt, defame, or offend anyone.*

I have a lot of memories from my childhood. There are some good and some bad. I grew up around my nieces and nephews, who were more like my brothers and sisters because of our closeness in age. Although I thought my childhood was typical, I know now that the so-called functional childhood was dysfunctional. My mom did the best that she could to raise me and five of my siblings. As a child growing up, I did not understand everything that I saw. My surroundings consisted of dysfunctional relationships, mental illness, sexual immorality, and drugs. As an adult, I now understand what all of that did to people.

I started being aware at a very young age, at least around three years old. I would see these things and think they were normal, but this would affect me tremendously in my adult life. As I got a bit older, I noticed a distinguishment. I felt like the black sheep, not only in my family but wherever I went. My family never treated me differently. My mom, dad, and siblings love me very much. However, I was self-conscious of my skin color and size, along with not having the ability to stand up for myself. My confidence was weak at a young age. It caused problems for me at school. I felt that I was an outcast in everything, and I did not know how to communicate how I felt. I did not feel smart, and I didn't know how to convey some of the cruel things that happened to me. It seemed like I had to figure it all out by myself.

I had never seen my mother communicate about the troubles she dealt with. I only observed high emotionalism. My father was around up until I was around five years old. I loved my father, and he did what he could for us. At the age of 14, he passed away, and that took a toll on me. I started having bad cases of anxiety. So much so that my PCP wanted me to be on medication. I didn't want that stuff, so I learned how to deal with it until I was able to learn how to conquer it later. As I got older, I recognized that it was the enemy trying to ruin me before I got started.

As I began my teenage years, I became promiscuous and wanted so badly to fit in. I knew something was keeping me from going off the deep end, but because I did not know who I was, I dated guys I wouldn't have dared look twice at now. My self-esteem was low, and I settled. I didn't want to challenge myself because, honestly, that's all I knew. My "friends" were drugheads, and most of them had children at an early age. I had a friend who stayed in the projects and had guys coming in and out like clockwork. She played porn in front of her children and allowed people to freely come in and out as they pleased.

Smoking weed and popping pills seemed like a daily thing. Let us not leave out the Bacardi, beer, and vodka. Drugs were not my thing, but I had my share of alcohol. Actually, I felt it was quickly turning into alcoholism. I began drinking around 18 years old, starting with the "cute" fruity drinks and then working my way up to hard liquors. Most of the people I hung out with were in their twenties, so they purchased the alcohol for me. Me and my boyfriend at the time, let's call him MC, drank hard, and sometimes we didn't know what was going on around us or where we were. At this point, I had graduated to 100-proof vodka. There were no more sweet drinks for me.

An event occurred that would stop all of this instantly. One night, MC and I parked at a hotel and were talking. I was crying, and still, today, I have no idea why. All I know is that we both were drunk. It was dark out and raining. Out of nowhere, I saw this bright light flashing through the window and heard knocking on the window! Then, I heard a deep and authoritative voice saying open the door!!! It was a police officer. I was scared sober! I tried to hide the alcohol under my jacket as if he didn't see me trying to. Just dumb. He proceeded to tell MC and me to get out of the car. I didn't know much about the Lord then, but I called on him that night! The officer said, "Don't be trying to call on him now!"

He went on to tell us that someone called us in because it looked like MC was doing something to me, but he also knew we were drunk. Side note: He happened to be an African American cop. I believe that helped along with the favor of the Lord (Just Saying). Backup was on the way, but he told us to get our "ASSES" back in the car and go home! I was so grateful that day. After that, I broke up with MC and stayed far away from alcohol. It is on rare occasions that I even fool with wine!

I felt my life was going down a never-ending hole. I continued to always end up with broken men but called myself upgrading because I wouldn't date anyone who did drugs or was an alcoholic anymore. However, dysfunction and psychological issues come in many facets. Sometimes, you do not see them right away. Either that, or you are in denial. Also, you attract what you are. That means I was broken, too.

Around nineteen, I started working as a dietician assistant at one of the major hospitals in Nashville. I wanted a change in my life but did not know how to do it. I ended up signing up for dental assisting school just to have a "new beginning" and to get away. Again, I was running. Looking at it now, I was changing environments, but I was not changing me. Everywhere I went, I ran back into myself.

Eventually, a new lady started working with us. She was quiet and pretty much kept to herself. It was something different about her, but I could not put my finger on it. Somehow, we started hanging around each other. Her name was Ms. Scott. She was an older lady and more of a mother figure to me. We began to get close.

Eventually, we started hanging out after work. She had three sons that I would meet soon after. In our conversations, I noticed she would frequently invite me to church. Honestly, I was not thinking about church at all and still wanted to do what I wanted to. Eventually, I broke down and went. The church was on Whites Creek Pike in Nashville, TN. I went once, and it felt like the pastor was talking directly to me. Did that make me return the following week? Nope. But after a while, it began to weigh on me to return, and I was starting to get close to her sons.

The church began to break ground on a new building in Madison, TN. Sometimes, they would have church services at a school until the building was completed. Around that time, I had graduated from the dental assisting program and started my new career as a dental assistant. I enjoyed being in the field, but it was short-lived. I went on to do something else and eventually started attending the church in Madison, getting baptized in Jesus' name and filled with the HOLY GHOST! The church was called Abundant Life Living Word.

Ms. Scott's middle child, who's one year younger than I am, would come and have lunch with her. One day, she talked about her youngest son wanting to go to prom. It was his senior year, but he was hesitant about going. I told her I would go with him. Side note… I don't know why I said I would so quickly. All I knew was I was excited to wear a gown and get all dolled up. He eventually became like a younger brother to me.

During the process of getting prepared for this prom, I felt like the red carpet was being pulled out for me. They paid for almost everything. I never had that happen to me. Eventually, I met her oldest son, and we were the same age. We needed a few things for the prom, so Ms. Scott and I, along with her sons, went to the mall. I wanted to look for some heels to go with my dress. Side note: every time Ms. Scott went somewhere, it was like a crowd had to go. I have never seen anything like that.

I found these amazing shoes, and Ms. Scott's eldest son wanted to pay for them. So, when it came time to purchase them, I was looking for him and asked one of his friends, "What is that dude's name again?" Why did I do that? They let me have it and teased me about it for the longest time, but he purchased the shoes anyway.

He seemed like the most mature out of the group. He had braids and dressed like a thug but was docile. His name was Patrick. After that, I was invited to Ms. Scott's house all the time. Eventually, I was with her daily. In addition to her boys, she was also raising her sister's kids. So, I would be at their practices and games. We were sort of inseparable. Eventually, I took a liking to Patrick, but it didn't go anywhere. He was like a closed book and had just gotten out of a long relationship. So again, I kept doing my own thing, but we did become good friends over time.

I would go on and meet someone at church and get married. I was around twenty-two at the time, and it would be one of the worst decisions of my life. The red flags were there, and there were plenty of them, but being dumb and naive, I went along with it. I mean, even in the early stages of getting to know each other, the Lord was trying to save me and make a way of escape.

On the day of our wedding, I dropped the unity candle. My mother had a stroke a few months prior. She was the one who helped me with everything. We would stay up all night making flowers, ironing tablecloths, etc. It was like all hell was breaking loose to get my attention, but all I could see was the infatuation I had. We were both young and nowhere near ready to be getting married. But, because we both were in church, I thought everything would be fine. It is such a deception. Just because you go to church does not mean that the church is in you. I wasn't even there long enough to allow the Lord to work on me. I was not ready at all!

I did not know all the hell I was about to put myself through. I take full responsibility for my own disobedience. The Lord warned me, and I did not listen! I felt like I was losing my mind and went into a bitter and careless rage. It was like I did not even know who I was anymore. I was apathetic and felt self-worthless. I did not give a flying, you know what, anymore, which could have cost me my life!

At that time, I had broken away from Ms. Scott and her sons. I was caught up in what seemed to be a horrific nightmare because of the decisions I made. We eventually got a divorce, and after that, the process of healing started. But oh boy did it hurt so bad. It was like that chart at the doctor's office with the circle faces when they ask you on a scale of 1-10 how much does this hurt? Mine was off the scale. I cannot even put into words the hurt, the embarrassment, and the drama I caused. We were not even married a year before calling it quits. It took about seven years to heal from everything that occurred, and the wounds are still there. I can say today, though, that we settled our differences, made amends, and went on with our lives.

At the time of our divorce, I was working as a receptionist at an insurance company, and I had to go to work with all of the weight of what I was going through. I felt like something had ripped my heart out of my chest and that I was dying every day from depression, anxiety, and fear. You name it, I felt it! I even looked sick, but one thing I did do was continue to show up to church and keep my face towards GOD!

I recall three men of God visiting our church, and they all told me to my face that GOD loved me and called out some of the things I was dealing with. Something had broken in me that day. The Lord knew that I didn't even want to live anymore. It seemed like everything in my life had come to a head, and it was like he brought a raven to feed my spirit and break a chain that the enemy had bound me with. I still did not do everything I was supposed to, but I knew where my help came from. I had also gotten back close to Ms. Scott and her sons.

I was so glad that I did not have any children and that they did not have to go through that process. I thought I couldn't have them anyway. I remember my mother taking me to the hospital at the age of sixteen because I was having urinary tract pains and didn't know what was going on. I was in the waiting room waiting to be seen, and a lady stared at me and told me that I would have a son.

I was shocked and said, "What?? Now???"

She giggled and said, "No, you just need to drink water."

Mind you, I had never seen this lady in my life. I eventually got called back, and the doctor did some testing. She returned and said, "You're okay; you just need to drink water."

I was floored! I held on to that word but continued with my foolery. AGAIN!!! I met a guy at the insurance company; I will call him Mr. IT. He was chubby and a bit shorter than I was but smart and geeky. He was an IT manager and could also sing! Sometimes, he would come to my floor for meetings and walk by my desk humming. He would speak and go on, but eventually, we started having conversations. I began to find him attractive as I got to know him, but there were those red flags again. First off, he was in the process of going through a divorce. Second, he already had two children and could not have any more.

I had fallen in love with him for various other reasons and was willing to look past these things, but there were definitely some non-negotiables, and something kept telling me to run again. We had started a relationship, and it had gotten deep. Eventually, I moved in with him. We were talking about marriage and options for having children. He even came to church with me and was baptized and filled with the Holy Ghost!

I really think he was willing to do just about anything for me, but that was the problem. It needed to be because he wanted a relationship with the Lord, not just to get me. But again, that does not mean we were supposed to be together! The emphasis on being "saved" was thick in my head, along with the "stability" he provided, which was dysfunctional. I had to really break out of that. We both had given no time to heal from the previous relationship and had no business even being together! I could hear my pastor's voice in my head saying, "Leave him alone and just be friends." So, I did just that!

I fought the urge and desire to see him in a way that would allow us to be together. I just could not go through all the hell that I just came out of again. At that time, Patrick had gotten married, but he and his wife had divorced as well. We had respected each other's space while we were married, but we began talking again afterward—as friends!

It was extremely difficult to cut Mr. IT. It was a stronghold that felt like the last big test before my victory. As I was in the process of totally letting him go, he immediately began talking to a young lady across from his office, and I mean, it was quick! That broke my heart very badly, but I recognized he was hurt as well. He just handled his by getting a rebound. I told myself I was done completely and got rid of everything that reminded me of him or anything he bought for me. He had purchased some Creed perfume for me. This is not a cheap perfume, but I did not care. I wanted it all gone! Unbeknownst to me, I was breaking the stronghold. Protect your senses! Some things can take hold of us merely because of our ignorance of how we allow things in our spirit!

I began to get into a quiet place with just me and GOD. I did not want to be with anyone else. So much so that I even looked at guys crazy for just looking at me. I had hit the point of "I'm tired of being sick and tired." I went out to eat by myself and went to the movies by myself. I worked out and began feeling so much better. I was satisfied with myself and finally reached a point where I was happy in Jesus alone!

I had moved out of Mr. IT's and went to live with my sister. However, I left my glass dining table over at his house and needed to get it. It was special to me because my mother had given it to me. So, at the time, Patrick had an SUV truck. I asked him if he would help me get my table from Mr. IT's house. He did not hesitate to help me. He came, and we went to get it. On the ride over to his apartment Patrick gave me a stern talking to because of how I was looking. He is a no-beat-around-the-bush guy. He will tell you like it is.

While I was out doing my thing, Patrick was working on his relationship with the Lord and was able to speak life into me. I was looking rough. I did not care, but he emphasized what I was dealing with on the inside was reflecting on the outside. He told me not to allow any man to put me in this place of feeling defeated. He began to speak words of comfort, and he spoke the word of GOD over me. He proceeded to tell me afterward that I was going to be his date at his brother's wedding. It was later on that day.

So, we got my dining room table. I did not want to say anything to Mr. IT; I just wanted my table and wanted to leave, but Patrick again corrected me and told me to be cordial to him. I did because it was the right thing to do, but I was thinking, dude, you're not my daddy. After that fiasco, I went to the mall and found something to wear to the wedding of Ms. Scott's middle son. I fixed myself up, and it was like night and day.

The wedding had started, and as I walked in, I noticed Patrick kept looking at me. I sat down, and one of Patrick's friends who sat behind me started acting like he was trying to talk to me and was teasing Patrick about it. I wasn't thinking much of it. Afterward, we proceeded to the reception, and everyone was dancing and enjoying themselves.

A song called "A Couple of Forevers" came on. I teased Patrick and told him, "I want to dance!" I knew he was not a dancer, but he reached his hand out to me. I was shocked as he led me to the dance floor because we were the only ones there. He said, "You know we are platonic; keep your eyes on JESUS!" He told me that all the time, but as time went by, I noticed the googly eyes wouldn't stop, and I thought he had lost his mind.

We got closer and closer, and eventually, we started taking an interest in each other. I had already spoken to the Lord and said, "Lord, you will have to confirm this yourself!" In my mind, I said how I wanted it confirmed; he would have to want to fast for three days! Little did I know the Lord had his confirmations as well! A little girl from my church told me the first one:

"You are going to get married on Christmas and have children for me to play with."

I told her, "Girl, you don't know what you are talking about! That is grown folks' business."

I then put it in the back of my mind. When Patrick and I were getting serious, we began to seek the Lord. I was not moving until the Lord confirmed it for me! So, one day, I spoke to Patrick while I was on break, and we were talking about our future together, which freaked me out. In the middle of it, he said, "Hold up! I am going to have to turn the plate over!" In my mind I said this is not happening.

I paused and then said, "For how many days?"

He said, "Three."

My mind was blown; however, I was still hesitant. I told him that was my prayer, so we went on the fast together. After that, we started to take our relationship seriously. It was December 25th, 2016, when he proposed to me, and it was one of the best things I could ever remember. It was around friends and family, and what the little girl said immediately popped into my mind. She did not know what engagement was but knew what marriage was.

We started going to marriage counseling, and Patrick even wanted my mother's blessing, so he asked her for it. The Lord continued to confirm. He was replacing the years I seemed to have lost and making everything new! On the day that we were to get married, Patrick would not go through with it. He was nervous, which was rightly so; we had both been in really bad marriages previously.

So, he went outside with his dog like he always did. He walked his dog, prayed to the Lord, and asked that He show him again if this was the right thing to do. He told me he looked down and saw this article in the paper on the ground. It had been raining, but the paper was dry! On the paper, it had "and they lived happily ever after" on it! We still have that paper to this day!

We went ahead, took the plunge, and went to the courthouse. That Saturday, we had a small reception at the Amqui Station in Madison, TN. It was such a joy! It was the complete opposite of everything in the past. After this, the Lord came through again! We had begun looking for homes and said we would not live together until we were married, so I stayed with Ms. Scott. She would take our apartment, and we would move into the house after it was built.

One day, I was looking at the floor plan we had chosen and labeling the rooms. On the guest room, I wrote "War Room." I did not tell Patrick this. He had got off of work that same day and came in with a sign in his hand.

He said, "Someone had thrown this sign in the trash, and I saw it and got it out." It said "War Room" on the sign! I was again floored.

I said, "I just looked at the floor plan and labeled the guest room that!"

The Lord was showing out, but the icing that took the cake was when I became pregnant. Patrick and I went on our honeymoon, and it was enjoyable. We came back home, and I noticed I was aching really bad, and it wouldn't go away. It felt like constant menstrual cramping. I never felt anything like that before. I took a home pregnancy test, and it was negative. I was not expecting to be pregnant because I never conceived previously, but I could again hear my pastor's voice.

We were looking at homes, trying to figure out rooms for children, but I doubted it in my mind. He said, "Oh, you're going to have kids!" After the negative test, I decided to go to the doctor sometime later. I described what was going on, and my OB/GYN at the time said,

"Do you think you are pregnant?"

I said, "No!"

He ordered a test anyway, and the next thing I knew, the nurse stuck her head in my room and said, "You're pregnant!"

I screamed, "WHAT!!!!"

I am sure the whole floor heard me. The feeling of knowing I was going to be a mother did not feel real at all! To know that the Lord saw fit and opened my womb at the right time was such a blessing! I called Patrick, and he cried on the phone. I had my little Josiah on December 24th, 2017. The Lord had confirmed all the way through.

Now, it's not to say we did not have difficult times. We had to go through the process of growing and maturing with each other. This process has never ended, and the enemy cannot stand against it. This marriage has a purpose. It is a kingdom marriage confirmed by the Lord. The vows that you say are a covenant. You will be tested on them.

One thing I do know is when I begin to doubt, I remember what the Lord has already done, and we press towards the mark! I truly can say that I don't think I would be here if it were not for the Lord. I was going to leave town to move to California right before Patrick and I began dating, and I was not even going to attend church anymore! That same day I decided to leave was the same day a word went out from the pulpit saying, "If you leave now, you're going to miss your blessing!" That hit home, and so I stayed.

The purpose of this story is to give encouragement and let whoever reads this know that all things are possible through Christ! I thought I was at the lowest of lows, but my GOD sat me up in heavenly places with him and showed out! I now have two children, and one with the Lord. I had a nomadic life, and now I am stable. I am an entrepreneur, and that entails being a childcare provider, a

Public Notary, and an Environmental inspector. Now, I can add an author. I am active at my church and with other organizations. My relationship with the Lord is growing, and I truly have the victory!

I have been to rock bottom, and now I can say I am a rock star. I may not have the education, titles, and notoriety, but the Lord recognizes me and tells me who I am! Oh, and Ms. Scott is now Moma Scott. She gave her life to the Lor, and look what it did for her! She has always wanted a daughter, and now she has three daughters in love!

Despite what you may have gone through in life, the Lord can take the bad and turn it around for your good if you let him. The Lord sees you from the beginning; he knew us before we were in our mother's womb and has a plan. The thing is, He will not take our free will away. So, in what you do, make sure that you are hearing from the Lord and being obedient. It will save a lot of heartache, time, and, in some cases, your life. Also learn how to be ok with you. Don't let being with someone be your life goal. When you find contentment in yourself, love yourself, and love the Lord, that's when He seems to move you along to that right relationship. To end, I will use this scripture: *Psalm 37:4 - Delight thyself also in the LORD; and he shall give thee the desires of thine heart.*

ABOUT THE AUTHOR - CHRISTINA KELLY

Christina Kelly is a believer in Christ and a current member of **ALL Word Church**. She is also a Wife, Mother, and Entrepreneur. She is currently a member of the **Women Who Rocks Nashville** organization and a volunteer at the **TPOM** (Tennessee Prison Outreach Ministry).

Christina loves instilling Godly values in her children and teaching those same values to other children under her care. She has worked in many fields but has always returned to childcare. She holds an associate's degree in business and has extensive experience in early education, but she loves being a wife and mother to her children.

CHAPTER 8
LADY OF PERFECT PEACE

MINISTER SYLVIA PAGE

DEDICATION

This book is dedicated to:

The loving memory of my mother, Ada, and brother, Richard, both of whom were raised in foster care. Their faith, perseverance, and musical talents placed them in the midst of stars while on earth and now in Heaven.

The memory of my father, Izell, who was proud of me, yet gone too soon.

The Temple Baptist Church family, that will always be precious to me. They live out the Christian love and fellowship that the Bible speaks about.

My children that I birthed, Camille, Robert and Dorian. God's plan was better than mine. I'm truly grateful for the love and respect we share.

The three men I loved as best I could, while I could. Through them, God intentionally drew me to him, placing me on His path to Peace.

LADY OF PERFECT PEACE
MINISTER SYLVIA PAGE

*Disclaimer ** The story told below is the author's version of life events as they took place. The author recognizes that other people's memories of the events described in the book may differ from her own. The details are not intended to hurt, defame, or offend anyone.*

It has been said that a woman was created with two internal voids. One void, only her heavenly Father can fill. The other void is for her man. I agree with a statement that I heard a television evangelist say, "It's often not our choices that bring us stress; it is our consequences." Even in my own life, that statement has proven to be true. Whether thousands of years ago or yesterday, whenever our carnal (selfish) nature emerges, it takes only a second to make bad choices based on an immediate craving or perhaps a physical longing. As my story continues, I hope you'll agree that God often saves us FROM ourselves.

Have you ever been taken advantage of or put in a situation where you felt you had no control, accompanied by emotions of insult and humiliation? Well, I certainly have. My first memories of deep disappointment and humiliation began between the ages of six and seven. My mother and father decided to go their separate ways, and I felt a rush of fear and confusion about what was happening to our family. I just knew my dad went from living at home to not being there. That resulted in my mother working two jobs, despite me having no consistent daycare. The solution was placing me in a well-respected children's home in St. Louis.

At that age, I was shocked that my loving mother was really leaving me there with strangers! I was scared and miserable. I was teased and talked about because I was a chubby child (my mother never said FAT), and I had very short hair. The girls in that home enjoyed finding ways to make me cry. Loneliness and confusion were part of daily life for me. I spent almost two years in that children's home under the influence of others, which caused me to feel ugly and abandoned.

On the bright side, I was the only child whose mother came to pick them up for weekend visits. Although I enjoyed those weekends so much, I would begin to cry when my mom had to return me on Sunday evenings. I lived with those emotions for a long time, even after my mother found an affordable apartment and brought me home permanently.

Inside all humans are the basic needs for validation, love, acceptance, and a sense of security. I learned later that God created us with these emotional needs because God's original intent was for us to crave and long for HIM. Unfortunately, if acceptance and validation are withheld long enough, many teen and young adult girls grow up to become women who are emotionally driven to satisfy those unfulfilled longings somewhere else.

There is a New Testament scripture that reads: *"Now I want you to realize that the head of every man is Christ, and the head of every woman is man, and the head of Christ is God." (I Corinthians 11: 31)* Of course, many women in modern society may take objection to that scripture. I do not. During creation, God made creatures with a purpose, especially humankind. I believe God intended man to love, nurture, and protect everything God provided for him, including a woman (which was intentionally given as a helpmeet to man).

From biblical times until now, women have an innate compulsion that drives many of us to please our mates and others that we seek approval from. The sooner we understand the truth about our unmet needs, the sooner we'll gain increased emotional stability. The deep attachment we feel to our significant others and the loyalty we invest in relationships can and often do bring havoc across our path. My own journey caused me to hold on to unresolved issues of acceptance.

I wore a smile most days, yet below the surface, I sensed that I wasn't worthy of happiness. As many of us have done, I decided to persuade folks that I would be valuable in their lives. I decided to accomplish a lot and WIN praise, recognition, or appreciation from folks whom I chose to be in my life. I began meeting the needs of others (family, friends, co-workers, church members, etc.), convincing myself that they would, in turn, meet MY needs and love me back. Have you ever tried desperately to blend in with a social club, group of co-workers, or family group, only to feel looked over and rejected? If so, you understand what I'm talking about.

Thankfully, we can apologize specifically to the Holy Spirit inside us for not viewing ourselves as God viewed us even before we were born (fearfully and wonderfully made) (Psalm 139: 14). I've learned that daughters need a consistent and spiritual male role model in their lives. Many daughters have a man in the house while they are in their formative years, yet the man may not participate in NURTURING that young daughter/teenager/young adult. Even with my loving, encouraging mother, who took me to church, hugged me, prayed for me, and often validated me, I felt something was missing. I missed the deep, comforting voice of my father. I missed his presence more than I knew.

I did well at school, and by the time I was a high school freshman in Indiana, I was often on the honor roll and enjoyed school activities, including the choir, yell block, and drama club. I dreamed of going to college to major in music.

My first boyfriend was Larry (not his real name). I was probably 14 years old when he began paying a lot of attention to me. Larry was a few years older, and I grew to like him. He was a regular-looking guy, tall and somewhat lanky.

Larry convinced me to allow him to visit me after school while my mother was still at work. I knew it was wrong, but I enjoyed being kissed and hugged by him. I said more than once that I was afraid of getting pregnant. His response was that he was UNABLE to have children. He sounded so sincere, and I believed him. Guess what? I got pregnant!

Going to the doctor and having the doctor confirm my condition was something I won't forget. I was angry and shocked because of Larry's bald-faced lie and knowing he didn't fully penetrate me. I was really immature and did not know that sperm can swim! I felt betrayed, and I wanted to pay him back for turning my life upside down.

My mother and I were living in a small apartment. She worked hard, yet she still fixed a good dinner daily and looked over my homework. She was proud of my good grades. There was no way I could add the burden and expense of having a baby in the house. That wasn't my mother's perspective; that was my perspective. Mama was disappointed, of course, and decided we would have a meeting with Larry and his foster parents. I was stunned that Larry offered to marry me! He wanted to do the right thing, yet I was horrified at the thought of being tied down to him at such an early age. I wanted to return to my regular life as quickly as possible.

Mama consulted our doctor again, and he told her about an agency in a nearby city where I could live until giving birth. An adoption could be arranged afterward through Family and Children Services. Mama never pressured me. She let me decide. At the time, I really didn't realize how selfish I was. Larry tried to change my mind, saying we could make it work. I told him I'd never trust him again because he was just a LIAR. I also did a lot of lying to my best friends and extended family. I told them I was moving away for a while.

For several months, I was away from my Mama again in a strange home around girls who teased and joked about me. Why? I loved to read books, listen to music, and write in my diary, prompting the girls to accuse me of "trying to be a white girl." Not being accepted was still a terrible feeling, and I had flashbacks of that children's home years earlier.

My daughter was born in 1969. I named her Melissa. The delivery was a nightmare because my labor came in the middle of the night, and it was a long drive by ambulance to the hospital. I remember screaming and gripping the hand of the paramedic VERY hard. By the time they finally gave me a pain shot in my back, the baby was there. Oh, my Lord! I didn't know I was to stay still for a few hours. Some nurse told me it would be alright to sit up. The headaches I had after that were terrible!

I learned a while later that Melissa had been adopted by an Air Force family. I felt guilty about giving her up and tried to convince myself that she was better off with a mother and father who could better provide for her. However, by age 16, I actually attempted to take my life. I put my Mama through a LOT. She was my biggest encourager until she entered eternal life and never talked harshly toward me because of my decisions. She allowed me to learn that "choices do have consequences." Some consequences are life-long, yet God truly forgives once we repent (Godly sorrow) and turn from our wicked ways (2 Chronicles 14: 7).

Have you ever heard the term co-dependency? It became popular during the 1950s when the 12-Step Recovery Program became very popular. Psychologists were convinced that while trying to shield alcoholics from the consequences of long-term dependency, family members and close friends actually developed their OWN patterns of behavior (sometimes negative behavior).

Family members and others would TRY so hard to assist the addicted person, that they began suffering from headaches, insomnia, weight loss (or weight gain), stomach issues, irritability, and/or other disorders. They felt a sense of panic when the alcoholic went on "a binge." They thought it was their duty to lie for the person, covering up absences from work, and making excuses to the children about missed birthdays, etc. To meet their OWN needs, family members took on similar behavior patterns of avoidance. Therefore, the co-dependent person depends on the person who IS dependent upon alcohol or another drug. You can begin to imagine how unsettling that relationship can get, right?

Well, before I reached age 20, I was living a co-dependent lifestyle (in Indiana) with my common-law husband. Bobby had a heroin addiction, and I wanted to help him save his job, his reputation, and his relationship with our children. I stood in the gap as long as I could, putting off college for a year. I was blessed to get hired by a federal government agency, so my friends thought we were all right. Not so. Even with my job, I could not meet all our expenses.

Daycare for two children was expensive, even then. Bobby kept making promises to "do better," yet I felt that old sense of panic creeping into me. I was really very tired and sad because I knew our kids deserved better. So did I.

After praying and having a big argument with Bobby (he had used our rent money to bet on a pool game), I decided to enroll in college and start again without him. Fortunately, as a high school Honor Roll Senior, I was accepted at Ball State University (Indiana) AND Fisk University (Tennessee). I talked with my mother, who knew my love for singing, writing, and stage plays. Fisk University became my logical choice for a college education.

The brochures I had were exciting, displaying that Fisk was (and is) a private HBCU long respected around the country for its history and liberal arts reputation. Since I had previously been awarded financial aid, I contacted Fisk, saying I was ready to attend as a full-time student.

I was thrilled to have a plan that would benefit me long term. I tried to convince Bobby that the separation would be good for us both. He shook his head, saying, "Things will never be the same with us." Of course, he was correct.

After arriving as a college freshman, I thrived on the knowledge and new experiences I gained! My precious mother agreed the children could live with her that first year. Wow, the new friends and freedom I had made my head spin. And yes, I had crushes on a couple of guys. I thought about pledging to a sorority; however, I decided to focus on my studies and singing in the Fisk Modern Black Mass Choir.

We traveled to other cities for wonderful concerts and church services. Part of me hoped that my absence would prompt Bobby to stop using drugs. We didn't discuss a treatment center because, during the 1970's, we didn't know of black men going to rehab. Who could afford that?

As I began my sophomore year, Bobby convinced me to let the children live with him (in Indiana) at his mother's house. I wanted them to spend more time with their father, and he seemed to be taking better care of himself. I agreed, and I believe Bobby meant well; however, he relapsed again! This time, the police pulled off a "sting operation" in our Indiana town, focusing on women and men who were buying and selling drugs. To make matters worse, I withdrew from Fisk University, caught a Greyhound bus home, and packed up my kids to bring them to Tennessee. Where did we stay? We had to stay in my dorm room for a while.

When we arrived, I thought my daughter had a bad cold (she was three years old). My son was age 5. A doctor at Meherry Medical College confirmed she had asthma. She breathed so hard that her ribs showed. I felt terrible that I couldn't help her. She was in the hospital for a few weeks. Like my mother before me, I began working TWO jobs to make sure we had a roof over our heads. We were also on food stamps when needed. I'm still thankful for the angels that were put in my path during those hard times.

By 1977, a couple of classmates kept inviting me to visit Temple Baptist Church. On our third visit, my children and I walked down the aisle to unite with that awesome congregation! What a joy. Over time, both my children were baptized at Temple. We're still members and still amazed about accessing and LIVING OUT the promises of God. Moving through life without a foundation of faith and connection with other believers would be much more difficult.

You probably think I learned my lesson and picked different types of guys for myself. Co-dependency is not a disorder that simply goes away. You must replace those negative beliefs and behaviors with real truth and new behaviors. It took me YEARS to stop thinking I could "fix people." I didn't realize that one of my unmet needs was to BE NEEDED. Be careful, Ladies. Many times, men can sense that emotion in a woman. There are some guys who will manipulate that unmet need.

In 1990, I met another attractive man, Eddie. We both worked for the same government agency. He had an almost Barry White sounding voice. He pursued me quickly. I thought it was an attraction, yet time revealed he was about to get evicted. He was setting me up to get him a place to stay. Did he tell me he had a cocaine addiction? Nope! He was smooth, a real charmer for a while. Again, I doubted my common sense and told myself he needed a godly woman like me. He needed someone to be loyal to him and lead him to a real relationship with the Lord. Listen up, Ladies! THERE IS A GOD. I AM NOT HE. Neither are you. Read that again.

I became Eddie's wife in every way but actually taking vows. Eventually, he stole from me, and I got him arrested. The stores he stole from also got him arrested. He begged me to make his bond and promised to repay me. He did NOT. Just like people with an addiction can relapse, so can co-dependent folks. You've heard the saying, "Take your burdens to the Lord and leave them there?" I was on that see-saw roller coaster of heartbreak with Eddie for 12 years! I could not save him, so I chose to save MYSELF.

I entered American Baptist College in 1999. A couple of years later, one of my professors saw me distraught one day. He asked if he could pray for me. I burst into tears and bowed my head. I GAVE UP my desire to "fix" anybody. In my spirit, with honesty in my mind and submission in my heart, I surrendered to the God I knew was real. I promised

Him that WHEN he gave me back my peace of mind, I would serve Him for the rest of my life. By 2004, God did His NEW work in me. He kept His promise to heal me. I'm keeping my promise to SERVE HIM!

ABOUT THE AUTHOR - MINISTER SYLVIA PAGE

Sylvia Page, affectionately known as "Lady Peace," holds the roles of licensed minister, counselor, published author, and event speaker. Nashville, TN became her home after matriculating at Fisk University, majoring in Music and English for three years. Sylvia's faith, her love for performing arts, her family, and others continue to be her motivators.

Sylvia's volunteer and work history spans over 30 years, including positions as a Receptionist, Teacher Assistant, Administrative Assistant, Personnel Supervisor, and Counselor. Within that background are ten years of employment with federal government agencies. She's an admired Bible Study teacher and event speaker. Sylvia has written policies and trained hourly staff, volunteers, clergy, and supervisors.

After being accepted at the historic American Baptist Theological Seminary (1999), Sylvia was most often on the Dean's List. She graduated with two degrees in Theology, minoring in Psychology (2002). Within the same time span, Bishop Michael Lee Graves anointed and licensed Sylvia at Temple Baptist Church, Nashville, TN. Under current Pastor Darrell A. Drumwright, she continues to give direct leadership to both Temple's Performing Arts Ministry and ACTS Counseling Center.

Minister Sylvia has counseled individuals and led numerous recovery groups, parenting classes, and seminars for thousands. She's received several awards and certifications, including as a Mental Health Advocate and Pastoral Care Specialist. Sylvia has advocated for vulnerable persons through the Coalition for Suicide

Prevention in the African American Community. She is an active member of Women Who Rock Nashville and Nashville Branch NAACP.

Sylvia produced and hosted a popular talk show on Comcast Access TV (channel 19) for six years. Her first book: "Loving Leah: A Legacy Revealed by A Woman Unloved" was published in 2011. Her popular first stage play was produced several times from 2015 until 2019. As a trauma survivor, Sylvia applies her spiritual gifts toward restoring discouraged and fractured souls. She happily shares the love of Jesus and life application of biblical principles because those strategies transformed her life.

CHAPTER NINE
A FORK IN THE ROAD

SAMAHRIA RICHIE

DEDICATION

I want to dedicate this chapter to my husband, Johnny, who is the most supportive person that I could ever have wished for in my life. No matter what the venture, he is willing to roll up his sleeves and support me in making my dreams come true.

A FORK IN THE ROAD

SAMAHRIA RICHIE

Disclaimer ** The story told below is the author's version of life events as they took place. The author recognizes that other people's memories of the events described in the book may differ from her own. The details are not intended to hurt, defame, or offend anyone.

Kelis… I reconnected with her when I moved back to Knoxville. We went to elementary school together and hung out in middle school. She was a cool girl, somebody who was just the life of the party, never really took life too seriously, and always had the latest hairstyle and the flyest clothes and shoes. Ever since I had known her, she laughed at things that were probably inappropriate, but she was very laid back and non-judgmental. She came to pick me up that night. Our plan was to go hang out and have some fun. We went and chilled, smoked weed and drank, and probably even did some heavy drugs. She asked me why I was with him and said I could do much better. My response was I loved him, and he understood me. He was my soul mate, and he wasn't all that bad. She just said again that I could do better.

When she dropped me back off at home, I didn't think anything was wrong; it seemed like any regular old day. We pulled up, and Melvin and his family were there at the house. The air was thick and hot as I walked in the door. He had been accusing me for weeks of sleeping with his sister, which I was so embarrassed about. I had been hiding this accusation from her and his family, but tonight, it would all come to a head, and I was mortified. When his sister heard it, they began cursing each other out, and then his sisters and mom left shortly after. His friend Shitty stayed. I tried to escape because I could see the devil in his eyes, and I knew this would be no regular night. In hindsight, I realize that he was severely mentally unstable.

As I ran out the door, I felt a large object knock me down onto the ground; it was a large 1980's Suburban SUV tire. He then dragged me back into the house of horrors where he and his friend sat across from me, with a gun on the table, and interrogated me for what seemed to be hours. He tells his friend to cut the stove on, saying, "This Bitch is going to die tonight." He grabs me and pulls me over, then tries to put my hand on the stove to burn me. He wanted me to admit to sleeping with his sister. It was untrue, so I never admitted it; however, in his mind, it was, and there was nothing that I could do to change it.

He beat me relentlessly that night. When I was finally able to escape to the back of the house, I called my mom's house but had to hang up, and they didn't come and check on me (I lived about 5 minutes from them). In their defense, I had a lot going on at the time, and they probably figured if they came over, I might not even answer the door. But that night, I needed them. I thought I was going to die.

I had long since stopped fighting Melvin. At this point, we had been together a little over a year, and he started the abuse within a couple of weeks of our meeting. At first, I would stand toe to toe with him, but he was over 6 feet and maybe 220-240 pounds; I was around 5'4" and 130 pounds. I thought if I quit fighting back, he would stop fighting me. Instead, the abuse became more and more brutal, both physically and mentally. The beatings finally stopped, and he made me lay in the bed beside him and sleep. I woke up super early and ran with just the clothes on my back to my aunt's home, which was two streets away. I left with nothing and didn't know if anyone would be there. Luckily, my cousin was, and I called the police.

They arrested him, but he ended up getting out of jail on probation (at the time he was on probation, so he was able to be released until trial). While he was waiting to go to court, he wanted me to not press charges, but at this point, I had already gone through taking pictures and everything. I ended up not pressing charges, but he still got his probation revoked behind the incident. During this time, I was still going back to him, so the judge sent me to court-mandated therapy; they wanted me to get help and find out why I would continue to go back to someone who was abusing me.

At the time, I didn't understand that I was addicted to pain and abuse, some may call it a trauma bond. Being a child sex abuse survivor, I had gravitated toward abusive situations my whole life. The therapy at this time was causing more hurt than healing for me. The sessions were 45 minutes to an hour, and you were expected to pour your soul out to them without the appropriate tools to leave and deal with the things you had just opened up about.

As a result, the therapy sessions just led to more drug use to suppress the pain of the things that I had experienced throughout my childhood, teenage, and then early adult years. It was very painful, but the drugs helped me to live and not think about those things. It led to heavier drug use and abuse of my body. I was also dangerously promiscuous and slept with men for comfort and security.

A year earlier, we were both on probation and living in a dark and grimy trailer on Dickerson Road in Nashville, where he was selling drugs. We were sitting in the trailer, one day and the police knocked on the door. He told them to come in without checking to see who was knocking; they saw his friend at the table bagging cocaine, which gave them grounds to search. They found small traces of cocaine, marijuana, and a gun, so they arrested all three of us. I was the only one with a clean record.

I was a tough girl and was a ride-or-die. When I was asked whose drugs it was, I stood on the I don't know offense, so of course, I was charged right along with the other two. My mom bonded me out right before Christmas with the agreement that I would have to move back with her to Knoxville. This would have been a great solution; however, I convinced her to bond him out, too, and he moved to Knoxville with me. I stayed with her all of one night, and then we moved into an apartment in Knoxville together. Shortly after, his family followed.

We went back and forth to court for what seemed like forever, but it may have been six months before we were sentenced. Since it was my first offense, I was ultimately given a probation sentence of three years with the possibility of having my record expunged if I didn't get into any more trouble during the sentence. He was also able to get on probation for these charges. This, however, was not an optimal experience for me; I violated six times during my probation, five of those times being for failed drug screenings and one time for domestic assault, which, of course, was dropped. I could not have a clean urine sample because I was addicted to things that made me feel good at the time; I wanted to be numb from the pain I suffered for years.

Melvin had started a serious relationship with someone else while we were together, and after I called the police on him, he packed up and moved out of the house. He was the sole provider in the home and had caused me to lose every job that I had. So, I started selling drugs and was making a decent income, enough for bills and enough to buy clothes and party. I was doing really well with saving for my bills, and I became more independent. When I got with him, I became very dependent on him. I thought that as long as he was paying the bills, he was taking care of me, and he loved me. I didn't understand what love meant at the time. I shared a lot about my past with him and how I felt like my family didn't care, and he played on that. He made me feel bad for wanting to spend time with my family, so I made him and his family my whole world.

He was sentenced to start serving his probation revocation time. Although we were not together when he was serving his sentence, he didn't want me to be with anyone else. When he was set to be released, I drove to Nashville and picked him up because I was going to make him come back to me. Even after what he did to me, I still wanted to be with him because "I loved him." Little did I know, while I was sleeping, the same day I picked him up, he left the house to be with her but returned right when I woke up.

From there, he would stay with her for days, then weeks, until he finally left me. I was a mental mess. Once again, I was feeling the abandonment that I was so desperately running from my whole life. Anybody, even an abuser, was better than the alternative of no one and being alone with my own thoughts and my own issues.

This time, when he left, so did I. I decided to move out of the house we shared, and I got an apartment. That house held so many bad memories that I just wanted to be rid of it at the time. I had a newfound sense of freedom when I moved out of that house, yet I was very lonely. I started dating or sleeping with a couple of mid-level drug dealers around town, and he did not like it. One night, while one of the guys was over at my apartment, he tried to break in because he was so upset. He ended up shooting in the air, and I was ultimately served a 30-day eviction notice.

During my stay in this apartment, my sister and her children moved in with me for a short while. While they were there, my sister and I went to church. We both went up to the altar at the service to dedicate our lives to Christ. For me, it meant getting baptized. I was so broken at this point; I was doing more and more drugs, and I just couldn't see a way out. My baptismal date was set for a week later, and during that week, the drug use continued. When the weekend came around, my sister said, now I know you are not about to go to church to get baptized. I was like, yes, I am. I just knew I had to do this.

The next day, possibly high and/or hungover, I entered the church and went through with my baptismal. I had a court date scheduled for about a week later, and I had to be out of my apartment in a couple of weeks. I knew that my court date would probably lead to me serving my sentence due to another failed drug screen. So, I started packing and preparing. When my parents came to pick me up and drive me to my court date in Nashville, we got there, and they revoked my probation. I was sentenced to serve my sentence with eligibility for probation in 3 years.

I was angry, sad, and coming down off of drugs. I also felt like I had to be a little tougher and have a hard shell to protect myself from possible predators. When I arrived at CCA (Corrections Corporation of America), I was in a program called Chances, led by a recovering addict who was tough and could see through the BS. I was hardened and didn't care, getting into arguments and being mean and uncooperative. I ended up seeing a mental health counselor at the jail and was prescribed something for depression and anxiety.

For the first few months, I was in trouble a lot; I would have to sit on the wall frequently, which was sitting in a chair on the wall in the pod all day. I could read, but that was it. I began reading the bible and other available literature. I read about Job and his afflictions, and after reading about these people in the bible, I felt like they were real people for the first time in my life. An inmate told me that I could get a shorter sentence and get out early by participating in Chances and asking the director for the fast-track program. I changed my behavior and was able to complete the program and get released after five months. I was released on September 2, 2004, and I have not stepped foot back in a prison or jail since.

I needed that time to sit and detox and have some space between myself and Melvin. All the times that he went to jail, I wrote to him, accepted calls, and sent money. He did nothing for me; his mom accepted a call and sent money, but he did nothing for me.

When I was released, I had nothing— no money and no clothes (the clothes that I had before going to jail were too small). I went into jail weighing around 130 pounds, and when I was released, I was at 180 pounds. Between the food and the medications for anxiety and depression, I had gained 50 pounds. I was able to get a few items from thrift stores, but that was it. This was humbling; just a few months before, I would go to the mall several times a week and buy clothes and shoes, and now, I had nothing.

The next pivotal thing in my journey was being on probation for another 18 months after my release. I was told I could not move anywhere outside of Davidson County, so I had to stay with my dad, who lived close to the jail. He did not make it comfortable and did not mind setting hard boundaries, which I needed. I stayed with my dad for six months and worked two jobs while trying to figure out how to get out of his house. I enrolled in school for Medical Billing and Coding at a local trade school. I rode the bus to and from school and work because, despite having a vehicle, my license was revoked, and my dad made it known that if I drove the car without a license, he would contact my probation officer. This part of my life humbled me.

During this time, I met my husband and got pregnant about three months after getting released from jail. Having my son gave me a new purpose and a newfound view on life; it wasn't just me any longer; it was me and him. My son saved my life because even if I wanted to go back to that lifestyle, I couldn't now. I finished my program for medical billing and coding shortly after my son was born, and I got my first real job. I started off making $9.25 per hour, and I was ecstatic; I also was able to get an apartment that was for people in recovery. It was roach and rat-infested, but it was mine, and I was over the moon proud of it.

I leaned into the Narcotics Anonymous community, and that was my saving grace for the first couple of years of being released from jail. I worked at that job for a little over five years and ended up getting my salary up to $40,000. While at this job, I decided to go back to school, got an associate degree in science, and entered the IT Field. With my credentials and strong work ethic, I went on the journey to find a new job. I would be fine until I disclosed my background, and then the door would be closed. I was stuck; no one would hire me because I was a felon. No matter how much time passed, it just wasn't an option.

Finally, a former manager left the company and put in a good word with the hiring manager of the IT Department. I was interviewed three times, and I got an offer of employment. After being there for a couple of weeks, I was called to the office and asked about my background. I disclosed it on the application, but it was an oversight during the hiring process. This was a God moment; I was able to keep my job at that company, received two promotions, and stayed there for five years.

The manager who hired me at this job was a God send and is still a good friend and mentor to this day. She gave me the idea to start my first business. When I was pregnant with my third child, who is seven years younger than my next-to-oldest child, I cried to her and told her I didn't know what to do and that I didn't want to have to miss all her milestones as I did with my other children. I worked hard when they were small to build a life for us and climb career ladders; I didn't want to do the same with this child. She suggested I listen to a podcast about a lady who buys stuff on clearance and sells for a markup online. I took immediate action after listening, and I did this the whole time I was pregnant.

When my daughter was around eight months old, I took the leap to quit my job. We also purchased our 2nd home during this time, and all the changes sent me into postpartum anxiety and panic attacks. This lasted for almost a year after having my daughter. The mental health issues that I had in the past were back with a vengeance, but this time, I did not use drugs; I sought out alternative things, such as grounding, walks, and talking about my feelings with anyone who would listen.

The business I had was starting to drain me financially and mentally as well. I didn't have much adult interaction since I worked in my garage, and I just didn't seem fulfilled. I also had to purchase products and hope that they would sell quickly to recoup the upfront costs. Although I made six figures in sales, it wasn't very profitable.

One day, my sister and I were talking about ways she could make extra income, and I started naming all these things. Cleaning homes was one of the ideas, and then I said, "I am going to help you!" So, we took up the quest of coming up with a name and getting a client. She came up with the name, and we gathered supplies from home. This was not easy work, but it was just what I needed. My sister decided she didn't want to clean after about three months or so, but I enjoyed talking to people and transforming spaces. This was another God moment. While I was helping her brainstorm, she was helping me find my new niche.

From speaking with someone who was going through a divorce, to an elderly lady telling me about her family and life, to helping the depressed mom get her home back organized, it was where I fit in. I was serving others, and it became a passion for me. While I am no longer in the field and speaking with customers daily, I do get to hire women. I get to hire the women who need a second chance, the women who are escaping abusive situations and need a livable wage to support their families, and the women who are homeless but, after working with us, get the keys to their own homes.

We are making a difference in others' lives; this is why I keep going. Because of my life experiences, I am able to come from a place of compassion. We have partnered with three nonprofits and are able to serve them through financial and volunteer opportunities.

If someone told me back in 2003/ 2004 that this would be my life, I never would have believed I would even be alive. Therapy and self-work have allowed me to grow past my wildest imagination. The day I went to get baptized and trusted in that plan was the day my life began. It was not easy, and it was not without struggle, but it was the pivotal moment where there was a fork in the road, and I could choose to go one way or another. I chose to go on the path that has allowed me to heal from trauma and help others along the way.

ABOUT THE AUTHOR – SAMAHRIA RICHIE

Introducing Samahria Richie: a dynamic entrepreneur, devoted mother, loving wife, and empowering business coach. Born and raised in East Tennessee, Samahria's journey is a testament to her resilience and determination, refusing to let life's challenges deter her from achieving her goals.

Samahria is the proud owner of Two Sisters Maid to Clean, a thriving cleaning service she founded with the vision of serving others while fostering a supportive environment for her team to flourish, both financially and in achieving work-life balance. Armed with a Bachelor of Science Degree from Middle Tennessee State University, she brings a robust educational background to her entrepreneurial ventures. Additionally, she is a dedicated philanthropist, generously contributing her time and financial resources to community initiatives.

Beyond her business prowess, Samahria is also a passionate business coach and mentor. She guides and inspires others to embark on their entrepreneurial journeys. Her expertise and guidance have helped numerous individuals kick-start their ventures and navigate the challenges of business ownership.

Samahria's heart lies with her family. She resides in Middle Tennessee with her five children and husband, Johnny, who serves as a pillar of strength and encouragement, fostering a loving and harmonious household.

Despite her busy schedule, Samahria finds solace and joy in nature's embrace. Whether unwinding on her patio or exploring the mountains, she savors the serenity of the outdoors.

Samahria Richie transcends the role of a mere business owner. She is a multifaceted individual whose life intertwines family, career, and personal passions. Her narrative serves as an inspiration, showcasing her unwavering determination, love, and pursuit of a fulfilling life.

CHAPTER TEN
THE JOURNEY TO "I DO"
(LOVE'S LEARNING CURVE)
DR. DEIDRA ROUSSAW

THE JOURNEY TO "I DO"

(Love's Learning Curve)

DR. DEIDRA ROUSSAW

My boyfriend initiated a conversation with my mom about taking our relationship to the next level, and he later proposed to me after keeping me informed. He was a commendable individual, consistently striving for personal growth, and I saw merit in his qualities. His intelligence, grooming, and independent mindset further solidified my decision to accept his proposal. With plans underway for the first major wedding in our family, an extravagant engagement party was organized, and my role was simply to attend. Despite my youth and lack of knowledge about wifely duties, I embraced the preparations.

During the engagement party, discussions about the wedding date ensued, settling on the following summer of 1990. Deep down, I acknowledged that I wasn't truly ready for marriage, feeling that we were too young. In that era, marrying early wasn't a widely embraced trend. However, I recognized my strong connection with him and anticipated eventually tying the knot. Although a family discussion generated excitement among everyone, I struggled to share in their enthusiasm. The news brought joy to my family, especially after the loss of my dad a year prior, but I was grappling with mixed emotions. Opting to align with the family's joyous program, I aimed for everyone to relish the celebration.

The process of organizing the wedding brought me joy, as I've always had a passion for event planning, be it grand or intimate. While my older brother was renovating our mother's kitchen, we conducted site inspections of potential venues for the ceremony and reception. Despite my mother's considerable financial investment in the wedding preparations, I began to have reservations. Feeling isolated, with no one to confide in, I sensed that something wasn't right. Amidst my fiancé's frequent absences, my suspicions grew, and the only person I could confide in was a close friend at work, a sisterly figure who was always willing to lend an ear and support.

A few days before the wedding, my fiancé picked me up in a rented car for our rehearsal at the church. I couldn't help but notice his new outfit, sneakers, and cologne, which left me feeling upset. Considering the financial sacrifices my family was making for the wedding, I was troubled by his apparent efforts to impress someone else. The revelation of his rarely worn cologne raised a red flag. During the car ride, we both admitted that we weren't ready for marriage, and we acknowledged the difficulty of explaining this to our families and the priest.

Upon reaching the church, we met with the priest to express our reservations. The tension was palpable as everyone wondered about the nature of our conversation. The priest returned to the church without us and declared there would be no wedding. The atmosphere turned hostile, causing emotional distress, especially among my siblings, who were deeply invested in the wedding. My sisters were in tears, and I struggled to comprehend their emotional turmoil. Witnessing their distress, I couldn't help but cry, realizing the pain my uncertainty had caused. My brothers were upset, while my mom, preparing at home for the after-reception, provided a bit of solace.

Requesting that we take a walk, my fiancé pleaded with me, urging us to proceed with the wedding. Faced with the emotional pleas of my loved ones, I reluctantly agreed. Returning home, my mother awaited me in her bedroom, concerned about my well-being. Tearfully, I couldn't articulate the source of my unease, suspecting my fiancé of cheating. Weakened by tears, I craved solitude until my daughter climbed into bed, offering words of love that comforted me.

The wedding day arrived, and I was a mess. Despite not wanting to marry a man adored by my entire family, I felt compelled to put on a façade. He, too, had reservations but for different reasons. In this charade, I missed my late father, the first man I dearly loved, whose counsel and support I needed. After the tumultuous events, my new husband was eager to leave the after-reception, but I clarified that I wouldn't be joining him, sensing that dishonesty would lead to future heartache. Amid my sister's tearful pleas, I eventually went with him. That very day marked our separation. The only person I confided in was my friend from work. While my family believed we were on our honeymoon, I stayed at another girlfriend's house, contemplating the situation and its potential outcomes.

Upon my return home, numerous messages awaited me from people attempting to reach out. One caller, a friend of my husband who was supposed to be in the wedding, rang three times, which was an unusual occurrence. Upon returning the call, I received heartbreaking news. When I asked about his abrupt withdrawal from the wedding, he hesitated, eventually proposing a meeting at a restaurant, insisting on a face-to-face conversation. I preferred hearing the information over the phone, so he disclosed that my husband was having an affair with a woman from their workplace who had attended my wedding. The betrayal led him to withdraw from the ceremony. All I could think about at that moment was the weight I felt surrounding the wedding.

I immediately called my husband for confirmation, and he requested a meeting later in the day to discuss the situation.

During our meeting, he tearfully admitted to everything, apologizing profusely. He begged me not to expose him, and I agreed, fearing it would make me appear unstable. He contacted his mistress to inform her of my awareness, stating they wouldn't be seeing each other again. At that point, my love for him began to dissipate.

Despite his continuous pursuit of me, he had spent money he didn't really have on the other woman. My family had largely funded the wedding, and he had driven around with her the entire weekend in a car rented for our wedding. To add insult to injury, he had invited his mistress to attend our wedding. I eagerly awaited the wedding photos and video, ready to confront this audacious woman who dared to be present on our special day. I was angered and prepared to confront his mistress directly.

The Tragic Loss of My Brother

Merely two weeks following my wedding, I received a distressing call from a neighbor. He conveyed the unwelcome news that my brother had been shot multiple times, and the outlook was grim. Stunned, my family and I hastily made our way to the hospital. Upon arrival, we learned he had been transferred to another hospital equipped with a trauma unit. However, upon reaching the second hospital, we were met with the heart-wrenching reality that he had passed away. Witnessing him for the last time, our close-knit sibling circle crumbled. The person I had always turned to for advice was now merely a memory. My mother, previously a pillar of strength, was devastated, having lost her youngest son, an experience that tore at our hearts.

My daughter, who had been with my brother that morning as he took her to summer camp, was the last one to see him alive. We never had the chance to bid him farewell, and the knowledge that things would never be the same lingered heavily. Losing my dad and now my brother within 16 months prompted profound questioning. I grappled with the perplexity of why God had taken two significant men from my life in such a brief span. With no one to confide in who truly comprehended my anguish, our family found ourselves engulfed in grief.

My aunts emerged as our daily pillars of support, aiding my mom in handling funeral arrangements. Their unwavering love uplifted our spirits during those trying times, and I felt as though they were providentially sent. On the day of the funeral, as we rode in limos towards the church, my family arranged for my husband to be by my side, hoping he could offer solace. However, observing him nonchalantly strolling down the street, it struck me that I hadn't even disclosed my husband's infidelity to my late brother.

Post the service, as everyone dispersed, the pangs of loneliness set in, and my apprehension of death intensified. In an attempt to find solace, I immersed myself in reading the entire Bible (KJV) within a few months. However, the persistent fear lingered. I yearned for someone intimately connected to God to guide me through these profound losses.

Prior to my brother's passing, I experienced a layoff from the Post Office, leaving me with ample time on my hands. Simultaneously, my daughter embarked on her kindergarten journey, and my ailing uncle moved in with us. Life took a somber turn with the loss of my dad, the passing of my brother, and the separation from my husband, leaving me emotionally drained. Despite the challenging circumstances, having the time to reflect on my thoughts amid my husband's bitter and distant demeanor post-separation proved to be beneficial.

While my husband made attempts at reconciliation, my reservations lingered. He proposed a serious conversation on a particular day, prompting us to meet at his residence. Prior to his arrival, I couldn't resist the urge to snoop around his bedroom, discovering some old phone numbers. Seeking reassurance that history wouldn't repeat itself if we were to mend our marriage, I confronted him upon his arrival. In his apology, he expressed genuine love for me. Despite his remorse, I found myself needing time to process everything, uncertain if his intentions were authentic or influenced by external factors.

Enduring More Loss and Unexpected Encounters

Just days after my brother's tragic passing, another blow struck our family with the untimely death of my uncle, intensifying my sense of despair. The relentless succession of tragedies felt like an insurmountable weight on our shoulders. Struggling to cope, my sister extended an invitation for breakfast at her house on the morning my daughter commenced kindergarten.

Seizing the opportunity for a brief respite from the chaos, I accepted her offer. Before departing, the photographer called to inform me that the wedding video and proofs were ready for pickup. Eager to examine the pictures and potentially identify my husband's mistress, I made my way to the studio.

Upon arriving at my sister's place, she shared in anticipation that she would watch the wedding video and peruse the pictures. As we delved into the images, the familiar face of the mistress surfaced, prompting me to revisit the discussions about reconciling with my husband. Holding onto the phone numbers discovered in my husband's room, I resolved to delve into an investigation. Deciphering one legible number, I dialed, posing as a friend from school. The gentleman on the other end willingly shared that the woman lived with his grandparents and even provided her schedule for the day. Stunned by the extent of the information, I called him back, revealing my identity. To my relief, he assured me there was no romantic involvement and that they were merely friends from the neighborhood.

Intrigued by this revelation, I agreed to meet him, armed with the wedding pictures. To my surprise, he recognized me, although I had vaguely remembered him from grammar school. As we engaged in hours of conversation outside, I found solace in sharing the burdens of my father's death, my brother's demise, my uncle's passing, wedding complications, and the separation from my husband. Grateful for the newfound peace he brought into my life, I experienced a joy that had eluded me for months.

As he prepared for work, he invited me to accompany him home. I asked to use the phone to apologize to my sister for not returning. Oblivious to his intentions, he stated to come upstairs with him to use the phone because it was in his bedroom. To my astonishment, his room was adorned like a romantic haven. Once I finished using the phone, I turned to go back downstairs; he grabbed my face and kissed me. I grappled with a surge of guilt despite my ongoing separation from my husband.

Disturbed, I swiftly exited his room, waiting for him in the living room. Upon his descent, he apologized for the unexpected kiss, assuring me it wouldn't recur without my consent. Our conversation persisted on the way to the trolley, and before alighting at my stop, he shared his job number, extending an offer to lend a listening ear whenever I needed someone to talk to.

Picking my daughter up after her initial full day of kindergarten sparked a profound sense of joy within me. She animatedly recounted every detail of her day during our walk home. The noticeable radiance emanating from me caught the attention of those around me when I returned home. Stepping out of my shell for the first time in a while, I offered much-needed assistance to my mom, who had just lost her brother that morning. Although everyone assumed my newfound joy was due to improved relations with my husband, the reality was that he played no part in it. My only confidante was my girlfriend, who shared in my happiness.

Reflecting on this delightful day, I decided to take up the gentleman's offer and called him at work. We engaged in a genuine conversation from 6:00 PM until 8:00 PM. After tending to my daughter and preparing her for bed, I called him back at 8:45 PM, and our conversation continued until 11:00 PM. He reached out when he got home from work at 11:40 PM, and our discussion extended until 5:00 AM. The following morning, after readying my daughter for school, he called at 9:30 AM, and we conversed until 1:00 PM. This routine persisted for the next few days, and I found myself developing feelings for him.

On Thursdays and Fridays, his days off, our connection deepened. One Thursday, he joined me for breakfast, offering much-needed company and lending a patient ear to my concerns. On Friday, he invited me to accompany him for shopping and dinner in the city center of Philadelphia. My niece graciously volunteered to pick up my daughter from school, affording me some precious time away. The experiences we shared were invigorating, and a special bond began to take root.

This attentive and considerate man exceeded my expectations. My husband and I lived separately, making my newfound love uncomplicated. My friend divulged that he harbored a crush on me back in grade school, adding an unexpected layer to our connection. Our love affair flourished, and he demonstrated remarkable care. This extraordinary man helped me conquer my fears and brought indescribable joy into my life.

Amid the confusion and inner turmoil, my family remained oblivious to the issues in my marriage. Always on the move, they assumed I was with my husband, unaware of our separation. The truth eventually surfaced when my husband contacted my sister to disclose our separation, a conversation I was not part of. Despite my waning feelings for him, I chose to heed my family's intervention and give my marriage another chance. My supportive friend graciously stepped aside to provide me with the space to work on my relationship.

However, trust in my husband remained a struggle, prompting me to seek employment at the hospital where he worked. My motivation was to approach his former mistress, even though I was aware the affair had ended. Navigating this challenging period, my husband and I made significant life decisions, such as buying a house, acquiring new cars, obtaining joint credit cards, and traveling together.

Upon joining the hospital, tension escalated as rumors circulated that I was searching for his former mistress. When I finally confronted her, she appeared visibly frightened, apologizing for the pain she caused, even though it was two years later. Surprisingly, I harbored no animosity towards her, recognizing that my love for my husband had transformed into something different.

Differences in religious beliefs began to strain our marriage, as I followed Catholicism while my husband explored Islam. In my quest for spiritual fulfillment, I grappled with questions about my purpose, evolving feelings, and the roots of my unforgiving nature. This internal turmoil triggered a personal journey in search of answers.

As my friend and I confronted the challenges in our connection, we found ourselves entangled in a struggle between right and wrong. Despite our sincere intentions, the feeling of being in spiritual warfare and the weight of our actions overwhelmed us. The scripture from Romans 7:14–16 resonated with our struggles, acknowledging the conflict between spiritual understanding and human weaknesses. We both yearned for deliverance from the complexities we faced.

Despite the apparent materialistic aspects of my marriage, a sense of incompleteness persisted. While maintaining a friendship with my friend's cousin, exploring different churches, dining out, and engaging in family activities, I couldn't find the completeness I sought. Eventually, after nearly a year of contemplation, I returned to my dad's family's long-standing place of worship and decided to become a member.

The growing radicalism of my husband's Islamic beliefs further strained our relationship, leading me to seek employment at a different hospital in pursuit of self-worth. Constant clashes over religious differences had taken a toll on my well-being, and I needed a fresh start.

In my new job, I was given the opportunity to train a segment of the staff on a new system. While the offer didn't come with additional monetary compensation, the perks were enticing, including free or discounted tickets to theme parks, hotel discounts, and rental car benefits. Utilizing these perks, I was asked to purchase discounted tickets to an amusement park for my friend's family. This seemingly innocent transaction became a turning point, creating a connection that rekindled our love affair and took it to a whole new level.

Yet, tragedy struck when my friend's brother was murdered, leaving him devastated and in deep sorrow. Having experienced a similar loss with my brother's murder four years prior, I empathized with his pain. Determined to support him, I stood by his side during the difficult times, further strengthening our bond. His courageous act of giving his brother a final haircut before the funeral deepened my admiration and love for him. This emotional turmoil created a rift between my husband and I, accelerating the demise of our already struggling marriage.

After the funeral, my friend begged me to stay with him for comfort, and I found myself caught between family expectations and personal feelings. Choosing to prioritize my friend's needs, I stayed by his side for what was initially meant to be a short period. However, one night turned into a week, then a month, and so on. While my family disapproved of my decisions, I was determined to pursue my happiness, finding solace in the companionship of this remarkable man.

In our deep connection, we decided to shape our destiny, fostering an extraordinary relationship built on love and understanding. Our shared values and desire for memorable experiences led us to explore various destinations, frequently visiting his relatives in Maryland. Our travels included trips to the Bahamas, where we forged friendships with locals and even became Godparents to a couple's son. Hosting Bahamians in the U.S. in the mid-'90s was a unique and fulfilling experience.

Despite the extravagant adventures, upscale dinners, and shopping sprees, I still felt an emptiness within, yearning for something more. The song "Why We Sing" by Kirk Franklin sparked something in my spirit, setting me on a path of self-discovery. Joining the church, I underwent nearly two years of counseling with a pastor who approached our sessions with stern honesty. This painful yet transformative process challenged me as I navigated unfamiliar church terminology and clichés, often accompanied by tears and tissues.

My husband and I underwent multiple separations as I outgrew our relationship, yearning for more. Our antics became embarrassing, prompting us to seek counseling for clarity. Through 40 weeks of spiritual growth classes, I discovered that we were unequally yoked, and I needed to redefine myself in alignment with God's calling. The counseling journey emphasized the importance of forgiveness for my freedom, echoing the biblical command to forgive others to receive forgiveness.

When I courageously shared my feelings with my husband, expressing the love lost due to his infidelity, a sense of liberation overcame me. We initiated the divorce process amicably. Exactly seven years after the marriage to my ex-husband, we divorced.

During the divorce proceedings, my friend, now fiancé, presented me with an engagement ring, symbolizing his deep affection and acceptance of all that I am. Despite imperfections, he proved to be perfect for me, and together, we embarked on a transformative journey.

Recognizing the emotional toll of counseling sessions, my fiancé scheduled a session with my pastor, who, in turn, developed a strong connection with him. This unique dynamic allowed us to receive counseling separately, fostering personal growth and healing.

My fiancé and I revealed our engagement a year later. While my ex-husband expressed discontent, believing in the high divorce rates for couples who had cheated and remarried, I was resolute in pursuing a future with the one I truly loved.

Despite societal norms and challenges, my fiancé and I saw ourselves as twins in sin, undergoing a transformative deliverance process. Our pastor and his wife played pivotal roles in guiding us through premarital counseling, even adopting my 9-year-old daughter as their Goddaughter. This marked a significant step as we became one of the first couples to undergo premarital counseling, with one spouse having been previously married.

Our wedding was a truly beautiful affair, graced by multiple pastors from our church. It was a divine event orchestrated by God. Our honeymoon in Bermuda was an exquisite experience. We spent each day with the parents of one of our pastors and attended their church service as Mr. & Mrs. Dwight Roussaw. The freedom in Christ was palpable.

A profound moment during the wedding was when our bishop declared, "It's you two against the world!" This became our mantra as we embarked on building a Christian marriage, fully aware that statistics suggested we might succumb to the divorce rate.

Several years into our marital journey, we received an invitation to join the leadership team of the Marriage Enrichment Ministry at our church. After careful consideration, we accepted the call. Recognizing the need to excel, the ministry sponsored our certification as counselors and training. Despite facing a challenging season in our marriage, we pursued additional certifications, including the ability to teach marriage classes. In 2009, we launched an outreach marriage ministry known as TWOgether Marriages, where we coached and mentored couples and hosted a ONE-OF-A-KIND Marriage on Fire Retreat, Marriage on Fire Radio Show, and the Date Night Tour and Experience.

Our commitment led us to be selected as one of the couples for the late Dr. Myles Munroe's annual tropical leadership retreat in Nassau, Bahamas. Witnessing the struggles of other couples, we conducted research and identified a gap: there was no outreach marriage ministry. Inspired by this need, we initiated an outreach ministry and, following divine guidance, established a comprehensive marriage ministry. In the early hours of the morning, the Lord always provided instructions on its structure, and a remarkable team of professionals joined us in bringing it to fruition. In obedience to God's guidance, we collectively authored the book "Marriage on Fire" as a testament to our journey and the transformative power of faith in marriage.

In a truly awe-inspiring moment, our Bishop S. Todd and Pastor Cleo V. Townsend granted my husband and me the honor of becoming Ministers of the Marriage Ministry on August 22, 2014—coincidentally, the day before my birthday. Witnessing the prospering of Truly Wed Wives in recent months, my husband received divine guidance to initiate a husband's ministry known as Husbands United.

It is a profound privilege to serve alongside my husband in ministry. God receives the glory as we counsel, coach, and mentor couples, and our marriage has flourished through our obedience to His calling. Celebrating over 25 years of marriage, we attribute our enduring union to the grace of the Lord.

On August 27, 2023, we received further licensing and ordination as pastors under the esteemed leadership of Bishop S. Todd and Pastor Cleo V. Townsend. In 2019, well before the pandemic, we inaugurated Union Outreach Fellowship, a virtual church—an endeavor inspired by God when we faced a void in finding a church to nurture our marriage weekly.

Throughout the undulating terrain of my faith journey, I have evolved into a fervent disciple of Christ. Weathering highs and lows, I stand firm on God's unwavering promises, trusting that He will never abandon me (Hebrews

13:5 b). In moments of trouble, His sheltering presence becomes my refuge (Psalm 27:5), showcasing His faithfulness amid adversity. My reverence for God has grown immeasurably.

In 2004, my husband and I began a journey of service in the marriage ministry. A pivotal moment arrived in 2009 when, during our research for the TWOgether Marriages ministry, God generously provided all we needed. Serving in ministry alongside one's spouse is truly extraordinary. It not only fortifies our marital bond but also stands as a blessing in ministering to other married couples. Our insights into the marriage journey are further delved into in our book and our upcoming release, "The Art of Forgiveness: A Forgiveness Project."

The saddest chapter in my life unfolded on December 17, 2014, with the passing of my beloved mother, Carrie M. Camp. She was my matriarch, a guiding light who imparted wisdom, showered me with love, and shielded me from harm. During this challenging time, my husband, daughter, and grandchildren extended their unwavering support, providing all they had to keep me going. Reflecting on how my husband covered me during this period only deepened my love for him.

As the Late Dr. Myles Munroe wisely said, *"Marriage is a good idea because it's God's idea."*

Now, let's delve into the crucial theme of forgiveness.

Forgiveness

In the Christian perspective, forgiveness is a profound and transformative act rooted in the core teachings of the Bible. It embodies the essence of Christ's message, reflecting the divine grace and mercy extended to humanity.

Forgiveness is intricately woven into the fabric of Christian ethics. Colossians 3:13 urges believers to forgive as the Lord forgave them, emphasizing the reciprocal nature of forgiveness and the acknowledgment of one's own forgiven state.

Beyond being a moral duty, forgiveness is seen as a pathway to freedom and healing. The act of letting go of grievances and releasing the burden of resentment aligns with the biblical injunction to love one's neighbor as oneself.

The concept of forgiveness in Christianity extends beyond individual interactions to societal and communal contexts. Believers are encouraged to extend forgiveness not only for personal well-being but also as a catalyst for reconciliation and restoration of relationships.

Strategies on How To Forgive A Cheating Spouse

Forgiving a cheating spouse is a deeply challenging process that often requires time, reflection, and a spiritual foundation. Here are 12 strategies, along with corresponding prayer points and scriptures to guide you through the journey of forgiveness:

1. **Acknowledge Your Pain and Anger:**
    - *Prayer Point:* Ask God for the strength to be honest about your feelings.

- *Scripture:* Psalm 34:18 (NIV) - "The Lord is close to the brokenhearted and saves those who are crushed in spirit."

2. **Seek God's Guidance:**
   - *Prayer Point:* Pray for wisdom and guidance in navigating the complex emotions.
   - *Scripture:* James 1:5 (NIV) - "If any of you lacks wisdom, you should ask God, who gives generously to all without finding fault, and it will be given to you."

2. **Understand Forgiveness:**
   - *Prayer Point:* Seek God's understanding of forgiveness.
   - *Scripture:* Ephesians 4:32 (NIV) - "Be kind and compassionate to one another, forgiving each other, just as in Christ God forgave you."

2. **Cry Out for Healing:**
   - *Prayer Point:* Pray for emotional and spiritual healing.
   - *Scripture:* Psalm 147:3 (NIV) - "He heals the brokenhearted and binds up their wounds."

2. **Release Resentment:**
   - *Prayer Point:* Ask for the grace to let go of resentment.
   - *Scripture:* Colossians 3:13 (NIV) - "Bear with each other and forgive one another if any of you has a grievance against someone. Forgive as the Lord forgave you."

0. **Pray for Your Spouse:**
   - *Prayer Point:* Lift up your spouse in prayer, asking for their repentance and transformation.
   - *Scripture:* Matthew 5:44 (NIV) - "But I tell you, love your enemies and pray for those who persecute you."

0. **Establish Boundaries:**
   - *Prayer Point:* Seek God's guidance in setting healthy boundaries.
   - *Scripture:* Proverbs 4:23 (NIV) - "Above all else, guard your heart, for everything you do flows from it."

0. **Choose Love Over Bitterness:**
   - *Prayer Point:* Pray for the ability to choose love over bitterness.
   - *Scripture:* 1 Corinthians 13:7 (NIV) - "It always protects, always trusts, always hopes, always perseveres."

0. **Embrace the Process of Forgiveness:**
   - *Prayer Point:* Ask for patience and endurance during the forgiveness process.
   - *Scripture:* Romans 12:12 (NIV) - "Be joyful in hope, patient in affliction, faithful in prayer."

0. **Focus on Personal Growth:**
   - *Prayer Point:* Seek God's guidance in your personal growth through this experience.
   - *Scripture:* Philippians 1:9-10 (NIV) - "And this is my prayer: that your love may abound more

and more in knowledge and depth of insight, so that you may be able to discern what is best..."

0. **Trust in God's Plan:**

    - *Prayer Point:* Pray for trust in God's plan and purpose for your life.

    - *Scripture:* Proverbs 3:5-6 (NIV) - "Trust in the Lord with all your heart and lean not on your own understanding; in all your ways submit to him, and he will make your paths straight."

0. **Celebrate Small Victories:**

    - *Prayer Point:* Thank God for the progress you make in forgiveness.

    - *Scripture:* 1 Thessalonians 5:18 (NIV) - "Give thanks in all circumstances; for this is God's will for you in Christ Jesus."

Remember, forgiveness is a process, and it's okay to seek professional help or pastoral guidance if needed. God's grace is abundant, and through prayer and reliance on His Word, you can find the strength to forgive and move forward in healing. In hindsight, it seemed as if we hit rock bottom in the marriage, but it was more like a downward spiral due to the inconsistencies of the flesh. Yet, my God stepped in with the balm in Gilead healing and put our marriage on a street called straight, making us feel like rock stars!

ABOUT THE AUTHOR – DR. DEIDRA ROUSSAW

Dr. Deidra Roussaw is a licensed and ordained pastor, certified relationship coach, leadership consultant, certified mentor, experience expert, best-selling author, TEDx & international speaker, honored by President Obama with the prestigious Presidential Lifetime Achievement Award, adjunct professor & dean of the School of the Great Commission Bible College & Seminary (Nashville Campus), visionary, blogger and the founder of TrulyWed Wives®, a wives leadership ministry offering wives retreats, seminars & workshops. She has a degree in business from South New Hampshire University.

Dr. Deidra is a Certified Sandals & Beaches WeddingMoons Specialist and a Cruise Specialist offering pleasurable resources and romantic exposure for couples to partake in for the purpose of strengthening and enhancing their marriages. She is also the brand specialist for the Wives on Fire Escapements, Wives Night Out ~ Slumber Parties by the Signature Wife Coach and TrulyWed Wives Society of Ambassadors. She is committed to providing exuberant experiences that will invoke passion and devotion to the sanctity of marriage.

Dr. Deidra is the author of "No Wife Left Behind" and a book she compiled with over 50 other wives titled "Wives on Fire!" She hosts a monthly Wives on Fire Mastermind and a weekly Wives on Fire Bible Study & Prayer Call. In addition, she is honored to be among the hundreds of women contributing authors of Black CEO.

She teaches wives how to create a luxurious WifeStyle and be their husband's GOOD THING & mentors WifeCEOs on balancing business and marriage as WifePreneurs. She is the co-founder of TWOgether Marriages, hosts an annual Marriage on Fire Retreat ~ Marriage Sailabration, a monthly "Date Night Tour & Experience," Editor-in-Chief for the Marriage on Fire Magazine, Magazine Publisher and the host of the Marriage on Fire Radio Show alongside her husband, Dr. Dwight Roussaw.

Dr. Deidra is a graduate and alumni of Success Mastery Coaching under the leadership of Dr. Stacia Pierce, Arianna Pierce, and the David Tutera Mentorship Program.

~Her Wife Verse~

"A wife of noble character is her husband's crown"
~Proverbs 12:4

CHAPTER ELEVEN
IT WAS PERFECT, UNTIL IT WASN'T
-A DATING NIGHTMARE-
TRUE STORY

ELBONY WEATHERSPOON

DEDICATION

I dedicate this book to all survivors who have overcome tremendous challenges, those who have fought for positivity, and those who strive to make a difference in our world. I pledge to be a champion of change for those whose voices have been silenced by senseless violence linked to mental illness.

- In the face of adversity, these survivors have shown remarkable resilience and strength, inspiring others to never give up.
- Their stories serve as a beacon of hope for those going through tough times, demonstrating that it is possible to emerge stronger on the other side.
- By dedicating this book to them, I honor their courage and perseverance, acknowledging the battles they have faced and the victories they have achieved.
- Let their journeys remind us of the power of the human spirit and the importance of supporting one another in times of need.
- Together, we can work towards a more compassionate and understanding society where mental health is prioritized and stigma is replaced with empathy and support.

ACKNOWLEDGMENTS

Thank you to my children, Millie, Zavion, and Isaiah. This is proof that you can do and be anything you want to be. With hard work and dedication, your dreams are at your command.

Life is what you make it…Nothing more, Nothing less.

#MommiesDreamsMatter #ProgressisaProcess

Thank you to my parents, Linda & Herbert Weatherspoon, and my siblings, Tabetha and Bubba

I wouldn't have made it without you. #Family

Derrick Jr - Thank you for all that you have done and all you continue to do. You are appreciated, and we Love you! #Family4Life

Asha and Kim - Thank you for always being there throughout life.

Friends for a lifetime. #A1sinceDay1

Q - Thank you for believing in me even when I didn't believe in myself. #Twin

IT WAS PERFECT, UNTIL IT WASN'T

-A DATING NIGHTMARE-

TRUE STORY

ELBONY WEATHERSPOON

*Disclaimer ** The story told below is the author's version of life events as they took place. The author recognizes that other people's memories of the events described in the book may differ from her own. The details are not intended to hurt, defame, or offend anyone.*

Introduction

Here's a captivating tale for those who are single and eager to socialize, navigating the dating world anew, involved with a partner dealing with mental health challenges, or exploring ways to vet a potential match. Meet Elbony Weatherspoon, who, like many, sought enduring love, only to realize that her Prince charming was not everything he seemed. This narrative delves into themes of domestic abuse, mental health, and law enforcement protocols, painting a vivid picture of a harrowing dating experience.

Her story begins with hope and excitement as she embarks on her quest for love, eager to find her happily ever after. She meets a man who seems to tick all the boxes—attentive, caring, and charming. However, as their relationship progresses, cracks begin to show. She finds herself walking on eggshells, constantly trying to please her partner to avoid his unpredictable outbursts.

As she delved deeper into the relationship, she uncovered the harsh reality that her Prince Charming was not who he portrayed himself to be. She discovered that he was struggling with a mental health disorder and was not taking his medication, which would cause him to have a manic episode that would leave her and her kids homeless. Although she called for help from the local police, she was hit with disappointment when she realized there was no plan in place for her situation.

Throughout this turbulent journey, she navigated the complexities of seeking help and support. She reached out to mental health professionals, sought guidance from support groups, familiarized herself with law enforcement protocols to ensure her safety, and engaged in community activism to change the gray areas of the three at hand: Domestic Violence, Mental Illness, and police policy and procedure. Despite the obstacles she faced, she remained resilient, determined to break free from the cycle of abuse and reclaim her sense of self-worth.

As her story unfolds, her resilience and courage shine through, inspiring others to recognize the signs of abuse, prioritize their mental health, and seek help when needed. Through her harrowing dating experience, her journey serves as a powerful reminder that love should never come at the cost of one's well-being, and that seeking support is a courageous step towards healing and self-empowerment.

Stay up to date on her story, new books, events, and social media at the QR code.

Chapter 1: Lonely Even When Not Alone

The Beginning…

When I say 2023 was a hell of a year…it was hell on earth for me.

I never would have thought I would be writing this book or that you would be reading it, so thank you for sharing your time with me. Now, before we get started, go ahead and get yourself some wine, snacks, or whatever your preference is to wind down because I have a story to tell you, my friend.

Now, I am a pretty private person, but I made a vow to myself to share my story in hopes of saving someone's life. If only I knew then what I know now, I wouldn't be writing this at all.

It's crazy how the universe works… One day you're living your best life, and the next, you're right back where you started, in addition to dependents, bills up your ass, and settling for a situationship; yes, friend, you know, those dead-end relationships.

You end up finding yourself working some dead-end job, putting your dreams in the trash, and your goals on the back burner. Your New Year's resolutions are as dead as a tree in the winter, and the people you never second-guessed are now being questioned. The people you love don't really love you, and the life you once wanted is a figment of your imagination.

In the cycle of routine, you wake up at the same time each day to engage in familiar activities with the same individuals, 5-7 days a week. Don't overlook the 365 days a year of parenting, alongside managing family, personal, and emotional challenges alone. Life is what it is, and it keeps going on. When work is added to the mix, you find yourself in a typical "This is life" Sunday scenario.

Situation-ships are increasingly prevalent nowadays, mainly due to the high cost of living. Relationships seem to revolve more around finances and work rather than love, support, or respect in today's world. Quite a thought-provoking scenario, isn't it?

In the past half-year, I've had to part ways with individuals I never imagined living without, including family members. I left a job I never thought I'd quit and conquered the toughest challenge of my life. Experiencing survival mode first-hand, learning to love and be loved without being "the one," and enduring the captivity of my own mind have all shaped my journey.

During my upbringing, I often sought love in the wrong places. However, as time passed, I realized that it was the powerful concept of "Generational curses" that steered me towards destructive paths in love and relationships. To be frank, I was uncertain about what love truly meant, but as I grew older, my desire to heal and embrace love, rather than toxicity and pain, intensified.

Growing up, I had both parents, but their relationship was as polluted as the water of the Mississippi River. All I witnessed was the love struggle. My mother prioritized my father over herself, tolerating the intolerable due to the emotional attachment known as love and a mere document. She cherished her marriage and honored the vows exchanged on their wedding day.

My dad stayed for our sake, for the well-being of the children.

But when "All for the kids" makes you unhappy, what do you do?

Do you stay? Live up to the vow for better or worse? Or do you flee to the next suitable candidate?

Never say what you won't do because, in the midst of pain and confusion, there is no telling what you will do.

I used to believe that pain equated to love. Mistakes followed by returns were seen as expressions of affection, and apologies after hurtful words were considered signs of caring. However, in truth, these were instances of unaddressed trauma that needed recognition.

Maybe if my parents had shown me genuine love, I might have understood what true love is, rather than accepting rejection and deceitful individuals as partners. I spent most of my adult years healing from the trauma passed down through generations. Perhaps if my grandparents had healed, they could have found happiness. On the other hand, maybe their healed selves would not have met, as they would have had higher expectations for themselves and others.

It was a journey for me to face the pain of my childhood. Discussing certain aspects was challenging, but I believe grasping how I've come to this stage in my life is essential. I'm opening up about this to explain how my parents' upbringing influenced their views on love, their expectations regarding love, and the boundaries they established in love, life, and the pursuit of happiness.

Their expectations of love overflowed into my heart, explaining why I loved intensely for an extended period, even when not reciprocated. I persisted in pursuing something that was absent due to my perception of love rather than its true nature.

"Love is patient and kind; love does not envy or boast; it is not arrogant or rude. It does not insist on its own way; it is not irritable or resentful; it does not rejoice at wrongdoing but rejoices with the truth." Corinthians 13:4

My Mother: My Inspiration, My Support System, My Friend

In all honesty, I owe so much to my mom for everything I have achieved.

During my childhood, I may have seen her as strict or demanding towards my dad, but in truth, she was fulfilling her roles as a wife, a woman, and a mother. Some traits that define me today have always been present in her since the day she became a mother to her first child. She has been a great inspiration to me, even influencing the song "Dayz Like" by me. The affection she yearned for was a void left by the absence of a father figure in her life. Having a father was unfamiliar territory for her, so the presence of a man brought her a sense of security. She desired love, protection, and financial security, which are fundamental needs a parent should provide, but she lacked them in her early years.

As a young single mother, she had to mature quickly and navigate the challenges of 1970s society, a time that must have been incredibly tough. Tragically, her father passed away when she was only three years old, as he was a victim of murder. In what way, you wonder? He was unfaithful, and the woman's partner fatally shot him, all while my grandmother was at home taking care of the children. As green as could be, she did her best to manage a household of eight all by herself.

Dating with children was just as risky then as it is now. Nowadays, we have access to information, apps, and telecommunications, but back then, there was no internet for background checks, no websites for seeking help, and no hotline to call. The fear of being judged for reporting a crime or feeling unsafe at home was more prevalent back then.

It wasn't her fault. Growing up in a large family of eight, she felt unseen and unheard, struggling with feelings of ugliness. These common experiences can be mentally, emotionally, and spiritually challenging for a young child. At the age of 12, she turned to makeup to conceal the world's imperfections, yearning for love. This marked her "Hell on Earth" moment. While my grandmother didn't speak much about her past, I believe she also faced love's pains.

Many people today undergo similar struggles. Understanding her childhood helped me grasp the cycle and the importance of discovering true love. This insight allowed me to connect with her as a woman and later empathize with her as a mother. I comprehend the depth of her love for my father, as he was her sole source of affection and support. If only he had known true love for himself, things might have taken a different turn.

My father was raised by both parents, but it was not as idyllic as one might expect. Growing up as one of seven siblings, he observed the missteps of his older brothers and sisters and strived to carve out a different path for himself. While my grandmother looked after the children and the church, my grandfather lived a more carefree life, doing as he pleased with whomever he pleased, which unfortunately included being unfaithful to my grandmother, a fact that was not well hidden.

The level of confusion and heartbreak watching your father ride past you with a car full of women just to come back home later that night as if nothing happened was the Weatherspoon household norm.

He discovered he had half-siblings while attending school. Imagine being at your locker one day when a guy approaches you and reveals, "You are my brother; our father is the same." How would you react? You might feel a mix of emotions – anger, confusion, frustration, heartbreak, and more – only to return home and try to act like everything was normal.

That was his way of showing love, believing that being a man meant taking care of the bills and pursuing personal desires regardless of the consequences. Witnessing my parents' relentless efforts to salvage their relationship was the most challenging aspect of it all. He engaged in infidelity with various women, some of whom were neighbors or familiar faces at the grocery store. I recall a particular incident in high school when I wore a shirt promoting our family business with my father's contact number. A woman approached me and eagerly mentioned recognizing the phone number, hinting at her acquaintance with my father.

With a chuckle and a shy smile, she remarked, "I recognize that number."

I responded, "Oh really, well, I'm sure many people do," subtly implying that she was not unique. The encounter utterly repulsed me.

My childhood was spent mostly with family members due to my parents' busy work schedules. However, those family members were not ideal either. I believe they were struggling with inner demons they couldn't manage, repeating behaviors learned from the past, and unfortunately, I was caught in the middle.

The images are vague in my mind, and as a way to cope with the trauma, I blocked it out; my therapist says that memory loss and childhood trauma go hand in hand. I can't remember what all happened. I just remember how I felt; I remember the smell of the house; I remember the feeling I felt being violated; I remember wanting to go home, and I remember eating to take away the pain.

Life was hard, and we witnessed it all…

With all of the arguments and cheating, my parents were never in a loving and caring mood; that was something we lacked in the household—emotional connection. I didn't know what empathy was like nor what a real hug felt like from my parents. It was like it was forbidden to show that you cared, or maybe they were just so miserable they didn't care to change it up.

I grew up in a small town in West Tennessee, predominantly white. I liked white boys because they were the only options we had back then; all the black people were related in some way. Being the middle child, I struggled to find my place, which labeled me as the troublemaker or victim of the so-called middle child syndrome. The pressure of not being seen nor heard and seeing my mother fight with/for my father was draining, so growing up, I always looked for validation from others since I didn't get it at home.

I used sex as a trick or trap to gain men's attention and interest, but it didn't do anything but remind me of everything I lacked. I was in abusive relationships that caused trauma, but I got it honest as my parents would get physical at times.

The last altercation between my mom and dad happened years ago, and it escalated to a dangerous point because I got involved. It was a moment that marked their last fight. The fear reflected in my eyes as I gazed at my dad seemed to be a turning point for him. Growing up as a daddy's girl, I perceived him as faultless and blamed my mom, although I was observing from the sidelines. Despite this perspective, I deeply care for both my parents. They both faced unbelievable childhoods and lived life to the fullest, with generational curses persisting on both sides.

Like many of us, I grew up in the 80s and was captivated by music—singing, rapping, and writing songs. My inspirations included Queen Latifah, Aaliyah, TLC, Mary J. Blige, Missy Elliott, and Timbaland. At the age of 14, I delved into writing and recording, cherishing every moment. It was my refuge from reality; I wasn't seeking fame, just the joy of writing.

Back then, without YouTube or social media, I hustled by burning CDs and selling them on the streets. However, after facing disappointments, setbacks, and financial strain, I took a step back to reassess my career path. I shifted my focus to pursue the American dream of health benefits and a 401k. Sadly, the tragic loss of my cousin plunged me into a profound depression, causing me to question life and my purpose on this earth.

In the midst of my internal struggles, I sought stability, permanence, and promise. Consequently, I entered a relationship with the father of my first child. Soon after, I discovered I was pregnant, and just one month after my daughter was born, I found out I was pregnant once more.

The struggles of being alone transformed into the responsibility of caring for my two children wholeheartedly, regardless of the other parent's actions.

After enduring four years of conflicts, deceit, and betrayal, instead of addressing his deep-rooted issues stemming from childhood traumas, he opted to move in with another woman and start afresh.

For two years, I had been in conflict with my children's father, mainly due to his former girlfriend, now his ex-wife, who had ongoing issues with me. Interestingly, she is now experiencing everything she wished upon me, laughed at me for, and criticized me about. While I don't find joy in someone else's pain, I do believe in the reality of karma.

It was just another letdown; my first real relationship turned out to be disappointing. I can't solely blame him for it; he had a difficult upbringing. Losing his mother at a young age to a tragic accident while she was on her way to pick him and his sister up from his grandmother's house left him burdened with guilt. With his father struggling with substance abuse, he lacked a stable parental presence. His older sister's unexpected passing during his high school years added to his challenges. Growing up without a father figure made parenting a struggle for him.

Our relationship had its share of difficulties, including heartbreak, letdowns, and even legal troubles, though I was only trying to support him. Ironically, I ended up getting the short end of the stick, but karma has a way of making everything right.

Tyler Perry once said, "You have to witness a person in all seasons," referring to experiencing the different phases like fall, winter, spring, and summer with them.

You should observe your potential partner through all four seasons of life, seeing them in times of financial struggle, prosperity, joy, and sorrow. Simply put, observing an individual through all the seasons of life allows you to grasp how they respond to changes and challenges. This insight helps you determine if you can accept them for a lifetime or if they are just a passing lesson.

I met Jr, my youngest child's father, a few years later. At the time, I was looking for stability and security within a relationship, but after the honeymoon stage, shit got real, and living together began to resemble more of being roommates. Over time, I felt trapped, realizing this couldn't be how life was meant to be. I yearned to be with someone who understood and resonated with my love languages, a concept I discovered five years into the relationship after a close friend suggested "The 5 Love Languages" by Gary Chapman. Despite my efforts to salvage it, it felt futile, like administering CPR to a lost cause where, eventually, you come to terms with the inevitable end.

I was aware of the gap, but I refused to acknowledge it at that moment, causing setbacks in my mental, emotional, and physical well-being. Despite appearing cheerful and showcasing my achievements, deep down, I felt like a failure. I seemed ok, but in reality, I was incomplete. I went from living to die, to really wanting the experience of what peace and harmony felt like.

Just a little about my ex: I was in a 7-year-long relationship with my youngest son's dad. Yes, he asked me to marry him. I have gotten a few engagement rings and proposals, only because we would break up and get back together. Although we had many good times, we grew apart. I always say either you grow together or grow apart in a relationship, and we were just two people trying to live and pay bills; as time went on, it was no longer about love and more so set on survival.

After my ex and I took a turn for the worse, we decided to move into separate homes when the lease was up. But not after dealing with yet another horrific breakup of him saying "F* THIS" and moving all of his things out of the home, including TVs, gaming systems, clothing, furniture, and anything else he could pack up in his car, just to move in with his mother. It did not make sense to me, especially when I never asked him to leave. But Jr. was just the running type, and after years of the same thing, I just wanted him to grow up.

I was open to providing a space where we could separate for a few hours whenever we had a dispute, then come back home to each other, sit, and communicate like adults. However, it was never that way. He would leave and decide to no longer contribute to any bills, including the help of our child. Knowing both incomes were needed to survive, he left, yet again.

That was the part I detested the most. The inconsistency and immaturity of this man and his family were profound. Times with him were literally like 'Night & Day.' When we were together and at peace, he would assist with everything, but whenever we faced conflict, he would separate himself and repeat the same cycle of disappointing actions. The responsibility that his actions required caused me to have a complete life adjustment each time he did such, which I resented him for.

I had minimal support from friends and family for me or my children. Getting the much-needed mental breaks, the time that all humans need to settle down and decompress, became nearly impossible. I was expected to manage everything because I was their mother, and I did just that! Therefore, when the lease ended for our shared property, it was like music to my ears. For the first time, he would have his own place in his name, and I would have mine, fully paid for without his assistance. I was prepared for this change.

I felt refreshed, embarking on my new journey. Balancing my full-time job that I adored, working out, and managing my business single-handedly brought me immense joy. I lacked a support system, however, and amidst life's chaos, I met someone who would reshape how I viewed relationships, life, mental health, and the idea of being there for someone.

In the interest of privacy, let's refer to him as "Epic" because he appeared when I needed someone honest and willing to provide factual feedback without sugarcoating. He acted as my accountability partner and truly helped me gain confidence. He was a significant game-changer in my life, but I'll delve into that later. Just know that by the end of it all, I found myself in a situation that felt like a relationship but lacked true commitment.

I loved that man, everything about him. Our actions mirrored relationship goals, yet he seemed uninterested in anything serious. I no longer wanted to be a choice; I craved a genuine commitment. Despite everything falling into place professionally, plans unfolding as envisioned, and life aligning with our dreams, there was still no official label or promise. Perhaps it was my mistake for becoming emotionally invested, but he was fully aware of his actions. It was all enjoyable and light-hearted until I found myself falling in love all over again.

After some time on the Epic emotional roller coaster, I reached a point where I realized that if someone isn't meant for me, no amount of love can change that. I made a difficult decision to give him an ultimatum—either commit to a relationship or take a break to navigate the heartache and uncertainty I was experiencing. His response that day nearly shattered me, and I can vividly recall it as if it happened yesterday.

Being in a long-distance partnership was undoubtedly a challenge, but for reasons I'll explain later. It became even more complicated when I asked, "Are we in a relationship?" His response would be hesitant, claiming he was 'quote-unquote' here for me but unwilling to fully commit to this relationship and be exclusive. I should've noticed the red flag and gotten out before the effects of another failed attempt at love set in. But it was too late, and the mark he left was a permanent one.

I was hurt, and all I wanted to do was be loved by him. Out of all the good comes bad, and a split-second decision brought me to the individual that caused my biggest shift in awareness and life itself. This sequence of events, though very nerve-wracking, brought about the woman I am today.

I reluctantly decided to jump back on the dating scene, and to my surprise, I ran into Mike. This man deserves an Oscar Award. He initiated the conversation, and our discussions unfolded seamlessly. After discussions on future plans, talks of blended families and generational wealth, I couldn't help but look at him and think,

Why is you single? (Yes, friend, I said is... lol)

He was exactly what I was searching for, so I thought. It usually takes a lot for me to build a connection, and with him being a fellow Virgo, our conversations were endless. After a few days, we decided to meet in a public setting. We spent hours talking in my car, making the most of the limited time I had.

Amidst the rain, he thoughtfully engaged with my questions, showing genuine interest in my thoughts and aspirations. His attentive listening and ability to echo my words back to me resonated deeply. We delved into our dreams and ambitions, and he revealed his passion for rap. A few days later, he showcased his impressive freestyling skills, which left me in awe.

Inspired, I stepped into a manager-like role, supporting his aspirations by providing tools for his endeavors. However, things took a turn. Witnessing a drastic shift in someone you care about is unsettling. Dealing with untreated mental health issues and the lack of proper intervention can be distressing. It's a stark reminder of how crucial it is to ensure individuals receive the necessary support and care they deserve.

When we met, he checked everything on my checklist. I conducted background, credit, and interest checks—all essential when considering a partnership with someone boasting an impressive resume. Everything was going smoothly. Dating was enjoyable, and having some "me" time while the kids were asleep felt great; dating as a single parent is challenging, especially without a support system.

Finding what I was looking for proved to be a challenge. First, the connection had to feel right. Any discomfort would swiftly relegate a potential life partner to the friend zone or beyond.

The modern dating scene offers countless options, especially with online dating becoming the new norm post-COVID. However, this can skip crucial steps in getting to know a new person. Being single after more than seven years brought its own set of challenges. Now, we can get to the real TEA in this story.

I begged for help from law enforcement because I feared for my safety as well as the safety of others while my ex was having a medical emergency (manic episode) that ended in him barricading himself in my home and destroying everything. Oh, and my missing gun, which the police refused to search for, although I reported it missing and stated that he was the last person with it.

Yes, friend… A true DATELINE Special Edition series…

Go on and refill that cup and popcorn cause the story has just begun.

ABOUT THE AUTHOR ELBONY WEATHERSPOON

As a Tennessee native and a single mother of three, CEO of Mommies Dreams Matter, Elbony Weatherspoon, knows first-hand the unique challenges that women face on a daily basis. This multi-talented revolutionist is on a mission to serve her purpose by helping others with her story. Her main goal is to shed light on the gray areas that she found within domestic violence, mental illness, and police policy and procedure. Her experience showed first-hand the disconnect when seeking help for someone in a mental health crisis who refuses assistance.

There were no definite protocols or procedures in place for her story, which could have helped tremendously. Yet, instead of being a victim, Elbony chose to be a survivor and help create the necessary debate about judicial change. Her story sets the tone for creating a platform needed to bring the awareness it deserves. This opportunity for change is not just for now but to help better shape the future for years to come.

Elbony has always had a love for solving problems, but this Virgo is using her trials and tribulations as a blessing for the lessons learned when sharing her story. She learned to embrace losses as lessons from her life experiences early on and shared them through music with lyrical content many could relate to. Now, she is taking a leap of faith to pursue her dream of becoming an author.

Her belief is that individual impact leads to positive community changes that are needed to change the world. Her motto, "Progress is a Process," keeps her motivated to achieve her goals. As a talented lyrical artist, she reflects the struggles of today's society in her music while incorporating real-life situations. She inspires women to pursue their dreams unapologetically and emphasizes the importance of self-expression and determination.

Elbony's book, "He Was Perfect, Until He Wasn't—A Dating Nightmare True Story," will be published in mid-2024. It is a powerful reminder that domestic violence is a complex issue that requires a multifaceted approach. Despite the challenges, Elbony's perseverance and continuance to fight for justice show what hard work and dedication look like. Her story serves as an inspiration to others who may be going through similar struggles.

In conclusion, Elbony's experience has made her a champion for change. Her ability to overcome obstacles and inspire others to do the same is a testament to her strength, wisdom, and determination to fix something that was broken from the very beginning.

CHAPTER TWELVE
MY RISE, MY FALL, AND MY REDEMPTION

A memoir of how I rose, fell, and climbed back up!

Stephanie Whitlow-Wood

DEDICATION

To my mother and father, Joe Earl and Suzanne Swett Whitlow, who never stopped believing in me. I thank you for never giving up on me, and I am so sorry for the pain I put you through. I hope you are proud of me. I love and miss you every day. I have worked very hard to become the daughter, mother, and friend that you raised me to be.

To my sister Angie, I miss you Every Day, All Day! Thank you for taking care of Mama and Daddy while I was going through my mess.

Thank you to my brother, Joey, for his love and protection, and who still harasses me now.

To my sons, Aston and Morris, and my beautiful grandchildren, my most precious possessions, you are the best thing that has ever happened to me. Thank you for loving me. You are my greatest achievement and my lifelong inspiration.

To my husband, my real-life Cupid, James C. Wood, who has walked every step of this journey with me since the day I met you. You made me believe I could do anything despite my past failures and mistakes; thank you for being my greatest supporter. Thank you for making all of my dreams come true. My Love Always.

Thank you to my cousin Cheryl Collins, My Ride or Die girl who has loved me since I was a child and who has been my guide. We were Grandma's favorite girls. Thank you for stepping in for me and always being there for me before and ever since I lost my mother and my sister.

Thank you to my Best Friend, Lisa Simpson, who loved me and stuck with me through my dirt. You are the one who knows the untold pages of this story and has witnessed my transformation. I love you, my forever friend,

Thank you to my lifelong spiritual leader, My Pastor, My Bishop, and my friend, Kenneth H. Dupree, for always telling me I could and believing in me when I didn't believe in myself. I love you, Bishop.

MY RISE, MY FALL, AND MY REDEMPTION
A memoir of how I rose, fell, and climbed back up!
Stephanie Whitlow-Wood

Disclaimer ** The story told below is the author's version of life events as they took place. The author recognizes that other people's memories of the events described in the book may differ from her own. The details are not intended to hurt, defame, or offend anyone.

MY STORY

To my Haters: When you can't touch me or penetrate who I have become, you like to dig up who I used to be!

Growing up in my family as a child was magical. On Saturday mornings, Mama would cook us breakfast, and we would get into the car and ride. The first routine stop for the day was to see my Uncle Austin. Uncle Austin owned a store by the name of College Hill Food Town. It was located across the street from Preston Taylor projects, and around the corner from Tennessee State University, then called North Nashville. Behind the candy counter, there was a tall man with large, bushy eyebrows. His name was Mr. Baxter.

Mr. Baxter would smile, give me the ok and I would fill up my sacks with whatever my heart desired. Sometimes, my cousins Susie and Wally would come, and they would fill up theirs too. Uncle Austin never said a word. The only thing that stopped me was the summer I stayed in the dentist's office; that cured my sweet tooth as a child,

After leaving Uncle Austin's store, I went to see Uncle Ben at his grocery store and then to see my Grandaddy at the old Swett's Dinette. (Save your wife for a pet and eat at Swett's, lol.) My Grandaddy. I loved my Grandaddy, y'all. I was my Grandaddy's baby, and I loved him so much. He always made me feel special when I saw him.

Uncle Ben also had a store called Swett's Food Market, up the street from Uncle Austin's store. He specialized in fresh meat, and Mama said he had the best meat in town. While Mama would be at the store chopping it up with Uncle Ben and Aunt Corrine, I would walk to the front of the building to see my Grandaddy. I was always Grandaddy's baby. He would shake me and say he was going to eat me up while I was little and sweet.

I would go through the line and get the largest breast of chicken they had, eat all of the skin off, and then go back to the store and listen to what Mama, Uncle Ben, and my Auntie Corrine were talking about at Uncle Ben's store. After that, we would go home and put up all the groceries that Mama had. Our family was very close, so my uncles would have the best for Mama. I love Mama. She was the best Mama and would do anything for her kids.

As a small child, I would mostly stay with my maternal grandparents. In my eyes, my grandmother was a beautiful, nurturing, God-fearing woman. She was brown-skinned, heavy-set, and very wise beyond her years, especially with numbers. There are numerous written articles about my Grandaddy but unknown to most, she was the mastermind behind Grandaddy's empire. My Grandmother never worked for anyone outside of the house. Instead, she helped my Grandaddy with the family business. She always drove a Cadillac, and she set high morals and standards for herself and her family.

Grandaddy and Grandmother bore nine children of their own and raised my grandfather's niece, Frances, who was one of the sweetest aunts you could have ever had. My Grandaddy was snow light. He could have passed for white, but he frowned upon blacks who would; he was too proud for that. My Grandmother said when she first saw him on that horse, looking fine, she knew he was the one she wanted.

My mother, Suzanne, a special education teacher and guidance counselor, was gorgeous. She was the baby of the bunch, and out of the five girls, she was the darkest one. She had three gorgeous sisters who were equally beautiful. All of my aunts were Miss Somebody in high school and college. They were noted for their beauty, and they were all college graduates with professional careers.

My mother had five brothers. The oldest brother moved to Canada after the service, but my other uncles all flourished and took after my grandfather at one time or another, having their own businesses. Women always talked about how fine my uncles were, lol. One lady said Uncle Ben was so fine that she and her friends would ride by just to look at him. My uncle David, who is almost 80 and still runs the family empire, is still fine, at least to me.

Life was good for my family. We were close-knit and stuck together. You were not allowed to show your emotions in public or air your dirty laundry. We were a proud family who the community looked up to.

When my grandmother Susie had something to do, I would go to my father's mother, Nannie Maxwell Whitlow. Her roots were in Providence, Tennessee. She was a tall, fair-skinned woman who was widowed. I promise you, she was tough as nails and as strong as a brick. In her spare time, she was a civil rights activist, and she had a strong belief in Jesus Christ. I used to hear her on the phone trying to help people. She loved her family, and in retrospect, I believe because my grandfather passed away so early, she tried to make up for it because she would always have reunions and events to keep her family together. She would be proud to know that we will celebrate 127 years with our annual family reunion this year.

She and my grandfather Jobe had five children who were also successful in their own right. My daddy, Joe Earl, an Air Force man, was a light-skinned, tall, slim man who was strict as hell. He didn't play; if he told you to do something, you had better do it just the way he said it. If you got smart with Mama or said something disrespectful, Daddy would smack your ass into next week for real. What I loved the most about my daddy was his presence during my life. He was always there.

When he became ill, I stayed home with him until the end. He never left me, so there was no way I was going to leave him. I thank GOD for giving me the strength and endurance to keep him at home with the help of my boys and Cupid. If he had run the streets and not been there for Mama, I wouldn't have. My parents had a wonderful marriage, and I am so happy that Daddy and I developed a deep bond. I loved the time we had together.

Out of Daddy's three brothers, he was the goody-goody one. One of my uncles worked for the water company. He was always sweet to me. He was the type of man who had multiple skills, and he was well-known. They say Daddy's baby brother was bad when he was young, but from the stories I heard, he was only mischievous. He is still alive in his 80s and a minister.

My daddy's two sisters were very ladylike women. One was a librarian from Tennessee, and the other one was a schoolteacher who lived in Detroit; when she touched down in Nashville, after putting her bags down, she would head straight downtown to Cain Sloan and Caster Knotts. She had several mink coats and always drove a shiny new Lincoln Continental. I was privileged to have two sides of family that you could be proud of.

Growing up, I was the baby of the bunch. I had an older brother, Joey, and an older sister, Angie, who always spoiled me; she treated me like the little sister I was. Angie took me to a lot of places with her, and she took on a lot of chores that should have been for me.

As I began to get older, my family members would tease me because I was the dark-skinned one of my immediate family. My brother always called me black bird; it made me feel inferior. When Mama and Daddy were out somewhere, my brother and sister would tell me that my parents found me in the trash can, and they felt sorry for me and brought me home. That made me feel like I wasn't good enough and never fit in. I always had people in my family who believed you were better if you were lighter. They would and still say horrible things about me, such as I'm too black to be my daddy's child. Thank GOD my parents never made a difference.

I still laugh and talk with these family members, but I know what they say. You can be lighter, but you better not be darker. Some of them may be educated yet are still ignorant when it comes to genetics. I don't care what they say about me. When I took care of Dad, we used to laugh and talk about it all the time. The only thing that did bother me about them basing their beliefs without facts is that it got back to my kids.

It was in my junior high and high school years when I started really getting bad. As a child, I was a badass, always getting in trouble. I was mean, and I manipulated my cousins and friends into doing things that I should not have done. In high school, I smoked mainly cigarettes, but after high school, I began experimenting with street drugs. I smoked weed throughout college and began to experiment with other recreational drugs; I dropped out of college and started to hang out with people who were addicts and who were also using drugs like alcohol, weed, crack, and cocaine. I was partying, drinking, and hanging out all night.

My life had no direction, and I was in a downward spiral. I had moved out of my parents' home, and I had lost all of the morals and strict upbringing I was taught; I was breaking my parents' hearts. All I wanted to do was try to medicate from my past hurts of never feeling like I was ever enough or like I didn't belong—a feeling of being misplaced. I was truly the black sheep of my family and a ticking time bomb. It was painful, and I was on my way to a path of self-destruction.

My upbringing afforded me a certain lifestyle that I loved, and others longed for. There was a trifecta of family, love, and unity inside my heart, my inner core, despite my feelings of being the black sheep in many cases. I grew up well, and I was well-connected. My love grew so intense for the finer things, the luxuries, the name brands, fun, and freedom that I became addicted to the lifestyle. With the desire for status and to belong being so strong, I had to maintain it. I was grown now, so how was I going to get it? I had flunked out of college, running the streets, partying, and staying out all night.

My appetite grew immensely. It opened doors and mixed paths with others living the lifestyle as well, no matter how they were introduced to it or maintained it. This exotic and intoxicating way of living crossed paths with people from all walks of life, from political figures and racketeers to business owners and drug dealers; these lifestyles appealed to me. Living this lavish life and being so open to others led me to a time in my life that could have crushed me.

The Beginning of My Fall

While on my journey of self-destruction, I met a man who would change my life forever. We were at a club out in North Nashville; I was sitting at the bar, hoping to meet someone who could help me support my newfound addiction, pay some bills, and buy me some Gucci. He was flashing money, and I was in the market, on the prowl. Unknowingly, he was out looking for a female stupid enough to set up, and here I was. I was at a place where a young girl with a bougie background had no place being in, and he and I hit it off in a platonic sort of way. He was medium build, brown-skinned, and unattractive to me.

There was no attraction to him physically. All I saw was his dollars, so the fact that he was ugly didn't matter to me. His name was William, and he was a cool guy to be around. Often, he would tell me things he wanted to do for me. He was talking my language because, at this time in my life, I wasn't working, so I was looking for an easy way out. William expressed to me his need for an increase and ways to make this happen, telling me that he would pay me if I would introduce him to a couple of people who sold weed. He said he wanted to make some extra money to support his family.

We often talked about ways to make money and bring increase and comfort to the life we were aiming to live. He asked for my help, and I willingly obliged. At first, it was weed; then, he wanted me to help him get cocaine. This guy and I would hang out and go places. Even though he was ugly, the money was good, so I started to trust him. Eventually, I would introduce him to my friends and social circles, bringing him further into my world. Everything seemed to be good until it wasn't. Time would reveal this guy was not at all who he portrayed himself to be. He had been using me to his advantage and getting all that he could from me for his career gain.

There was always something suspicious about him. I have always been resourceful, and I wanted to find out more about him and who he really was. The telephone system had just come out with *69, so I told myself I was going to use it the next time he called. Well, I did... when I *69'd his phone, the man who answered said, "VICE Hunter." I said what??? At first, I thought I was dreaming; I hung up the phone and redialed the number again. In disbelief, the same man answered again, saying, "Vice Hunter." I then became extremely scared and called a friend, Danny B.

Danny B was probably the biggest drug dealer in the state, with connections that even the police didn't have. I told him what happened, and he did an investigation. When Danny called me back, he had the guy's true identity and real name; he even told me where he was from and that he was a State Trooper working on a special task force. He had lied about everything the whole time.

One of my close friends is from the same town he was from, so I told him about it, and his family knew exactly who he was. I blew his cover, calling everyone I had introduced him to and telling them who he was. I called Mico, Sammy, Keisha, and Big D and told them all that I was sorry, but the guy that I turned them on to was Vice.

When his identity was exposed, I found myself at the center of controversy, misunderstanding, and embarrassment. When it was time for court, almost everyone who I had turned him on to was charged as well. Not everyone, since some people they couldn't prove, and there was no way I was going to tell them who they were.

During my sentencing, I received 7 ½ years. My mother passed out in the courtroom; it was a death sentence to me. The newspaper said I was numb and shocked, to say the least. After I had been sentenced and led out of the courtroom in handcuffs and shackles, a man came up and asked how I got the information on him being the Vice. I had already been given my sentence, so I made up a name. No way was I going to snitch on Danny B and say where I got that information. Despite what anyone says, GOD is my witness; I never told on anyone. I had already done enough damage to hurt others. The people who were also arrested were now my co-defendants who had been friends with me. I ruined their lives, too.

This guy had been given first-hand access to my life and lifestyle. Because I knew who he was and had blown his cover, he wanted to nail me and embarrass my family's squeaky-clean reputation. I had considered him a friend, so he had a bird's eye view and insight that landed me behind bars with a conviction and a sentence that scared me straight! This downfall was an embarrassment and shameful to me and my family members.

Suddenly, I was isolated with no labels, unseasoned food, bare accommodations, and minimal accessories. This is where my transformation started to begin—my revelation. While incarcerated, I had plenty of time to think about the most important things in my life and how to make my "come back." I began to reevaluate my life and realized that my poor decisions had affected other people and their lives, too. I decided that I needed to make changes and fast because the life I was now living was not for me, and though I had been sentenced, it wasn't forever.

While locked up, I turned inward during my solitude, and I got intentional with praying, reading scriptures, and planning for the life I was going to live upon my release. I had to show my parents and my family that I was done with living a life of crime. I focused on Habakkuk 2 verse 2, which reads, *"And the Lord answered me and said, Write the vision, and make it plain on the tables, that he may run that read it."* I took this to heart and began writing my vision for the life I wanted after incarceration.

It included marriage, kids, finding employment, and regaining and rebuilding trust with my family and friends, which were now my priorities. Although I still looked forward to the finer things, I knew many of the things that came with that lifestyle were no longer my interest or, should I say, my cup of tea. I wanted to start over, slow down, make some changes, and operate with discernment starting immediately.

In a very unexpected turn of events, I was released early. After serving four months of a 7-year conviction, I was given a suspended sentence and sent home. I made a vow 33 years ago to never go back, and I have stayed true to myself and my vision.

Upon my release, I put my past behind me, changed my lifestyle, and really started to find my purpose. I had been through some things, overcame some of my toughest battles, and made it through some of my roughest storms. Through the hurt, guilt, and shame, I was able to weather one of the toughest times of my life. I learned a valuable lesson about how my bad choices affected not only me but my family, too.

The Comeback

I graduated with a bachelor's degree from Tennessee State University and received a Master's degree in Public Administration from Cumberland University. I raised two fine young men as a divorced single parent. Being a single mother and losing my mother while my babies were young changed me. Internally, I was a different person. GOD purged all of the evilness and hatred out of me that I had as a child. He took my mother and my sister, and he gave me Grace and Mercy.

GOD blessed me with a good church family and a well-connected Pastor. I raised my kids under Bishop Kenneth Dupree's ministry. Bishop always encouraged me and helped me stay afloat mentally, telling me I was going to be serving GOD in a larger capacity someday. He always placed me in leadership positions at church, and that kept me grounded and sane while I was single and raising my kids. I really appreciated him seeing things in me that I couldn't see for myself.

In this life of uncertainty and through all of my guilt, shame, and pain, I was able to find love again. While being single for several years, I again reverted back to the bible verse in Habakkuk 2:2-3 and had written a vision of the man I wanted; I was specific, too. I told GOD I wanted him to be a regular, hard-working man who loved GOD and Jesus; I even told GOD where I wanted him to work. I began to trust and pray over my vision, not dating at all but just trusting that GOD would hear me and answer my prayer, 'Lord, please bring me a man who loves you, me, and my children.'

It was 2009, and as the season was changing, spring was coming in. Angie had become sick and was diagnosed with terminal cancer. Again, I had to rely on my two friends, Grace and Mercy. I found myself in disbelief and pain, not knowing what to do. GOD was preparing me.

I wasn't ready to lose my sister; she was my mother, my sounding block, my strength, my ride-or-die. Who was going to help me with my boys? Joey had moved to Florida. My grandmother used to say GOD won't take away something without replacing it with something.

After leaving Angie's one night and going out for a much-needed break, I stopped at the biker bar I often frequented. When I walked in, I spotted a tall, thin man. I immediately told my cousin Lynn…I want him. Well, before I could get to him, he approached me. Needless to say, we have been together ever since.

When I met Cupid, he told me he was a minister but no longer practicing ministry. He was broken then, and so was I. He had recently lost his family through divorce, and I was losing my big sister, who did everything for me. Well, at the beginning of summer, we buried Angie; I thought I was going to die! I was so broken, but I couldn't show my emotions. I am a silent sufferer. My boys were hurting, too, so I chose strength and suppressed my grief. Once again, Grace and Mercy carried me through

I was forced to accept the position of Matriarch in my immediate family. I took the position and took care of my daddy seven months after losing Angie until he went home to be with GOD and Mama. After Daddy was gone, I went back to work working with addicted women. The need to help others was still in my heart, but the vision was still being birthed. I wanted to help more people and share the love of Jesus Christ with as many as I possibly could.

In 2000, during Covid, I was furloughed from work, and so was Cupid. Cupid had been at Nissan for 29 years. He was unhappy, tired of his job, and ready to retire. I didn't really want to go back to work for someone else. Cupid didn't care if I worked or not; he always told me I should start my own business. So again, the need to help others began to race through my mind; even though I had met my soul mate professionally, I wasn't happy. With all of the education I had, I was still dissatisfied with my career.

I struggled with employment because of the felony I had on my record; very few people wanted to hire me. I even worked at a fast-food restaurant once with a Master's degree to feed my kids and pay my bills. I would work for companies that used or never paid me for my worth. I even had a supervisor tell me I was never a self-starter, as my resume stated. Despite the obstacles, I still had a vision. I wasn't going to let the white woman who looked like George Washington break or define me.

I knew that I wanted to one day have a recovery house. I wanted to give back to my community. GOD told me one night in a vision to open a recovery house and help men. I shared the vision with Cupid, and he agreed. I told him with my years of experience with social work and his background in ministry, we could help others; at that time, my youngest son had just gotten his real estate license, and he began to look for a house for us to use. GOD took us from our Madison house and put us in a larger home in Hermitage. We were able to take the home we lived in and make a recovery home. Cupid and I truly believe that anybody can be changed and delivered.

We transformed our home into a transitional home for those needing a clean, safe, and sober place to stay while being reintroduced to the community and societal living. Although misled before in my life, I can now help others not to make the same mistakes I made. We show men how to rebuild their lives. I found my purpose in life through my pain, shame, and guilt.

Now, I want to help others get through difficult times, too. I tell the men I help that their past does not define them and that they can do and be whatever they aspire to be. Cupid tells them the word and points out to them that we are all ministers of Christ, and God has given us all a gift. We chose to help men because they are the underdogs, the underserved, and sometimes even the forgotten. I am still on a path to help anybody looking to help themselves for the better.

There are restrictions on who is accepted into our homes. You must be clean, sober, willing to work, and willing to study the word of GOD. Everyone enrolled in our program is granted services to assist them on their personal journeys. Those who reside in our homes must be good (respect the homes and others and do their part) or be gone for the safety, support, and convenience of others. At Cupid Homes and our non-profit Cupids Transitional Care (I named the business because of Cupid's love for me and the love we have for GOD and others), we take pride in creating a Christian-based, family-oriented, clean, safe, supportive, judgment-free space that can easily be home to these residents. What sets me apart is my dedication and passion for what we do.

Since the conception of our business, the saddest part has been that we have never been approved or selected for funding. We fund our business with personal finances. I pray for the day when I can take these men out for steak dinners and show them the finer things in life or be able to take them all on a fishing trip. I also pray that one day, I will get help and assistance to help someone despite their inability to pay. Plus, I would love a staff to help me.

God continues to give me the means to expand and help others, and I have faith that one day, someone will see me for who I am now and what Cupid and I are trying to accomplish and help us. Until then, I will stay on the battlefield, taking in as many men as possible and saving as many lives as possible.

I may have never found my purpose had I not ended up behind bars with alone time to write my vision. That unfortunate incident almost broke me, but it led me to my purpose of becoming a beacon of light and a ray of hope for others as I live boldly to exemplify Christ on earth to as many as I possibly can. Before my incarceration, I had no purpose. Now, I continue to strive to become better. I can never turn back because of my two friends, who still hold my hand and guide me, Grace and Mercy.

My husband and I currently own and operate (4) four recovery homes in the Nashville and Madison, Tennessee areas. We aspire to open more and lead more people to recovery through the love and relationship with Jesus Christ. If you would like to donate, learn more, or become a volunteer, contact us at 615-853-2653.

Website: Cupidministries.org

Email: cupidministries@gmail.com

ABOUT THE AUTHOR

STEPHANIE WHITLOW-WOOD

Stephanie Whitlow-Wood, Co-Founder and CEO of Cupid Homes and Cupids Transitional Care, earned a Bachelor of Science degree in Social Work from Tennessee State University and a Master of Science degree in Public Administration from Cumberland University. She is also Certified in MRT, Moral Recognition Therapy and Trauma.

Stephanie has made it her life's work to support families and individuals who are re-entering our community after traumatizing or life-altering experiences. Many of her clients have survived tragic circumstances and need a safe space to rebuild and grow. Stephanie, together with her husband and co-founder Pastor Cupid Wood, make up the small caring staff at Cupid Homes and Cupids Transitional Care. They provide housing steeped in a Christian environment that promotes sober living and hope for an independent future. Pastor Cupid leads weekly church services for residents as they work toward healing and the renewal of their faith.

Stephanie routinely provides counseling to individuals experiencing anxiety, depression, drug and alcohol addictions, as well as those diagnosed with schizophrenia and bipolar disorder. The goal is to provide individuals with tools to help them thrive despite their challenges. Stephanie believes that the client is the true expert in their own life and sees herself as a compassionate guide and mentor to assist individuals and families in their recovery. She understands the commitment needed to rebuild and offers non-judgmental and holistic treatment options for her clients.

Stephanie is very family-oriented and comes from a large, loving extended family. In fact, at age nine, she began helping her grandmother to prepare family meals. She spent lots of time with her maternal grandparents, Walter and Susie Swett, founders of Swett's Restaurant, now in its 69th year of operation. Stephanie still uses many of her grandmother's recipes today when she entertains her family and friends at social gatherings.

Stephanie is a fourth-generation Nashvillian, and her family has long worked to make the city a better one—whether through education, civil rights, or the political process. She has worked on several successful campaigns in Metro Nashville and has served in several capacities, including field manager. She continues to collaborate with local organizations to fight for freedom and equality, especially those who have lost their rights after having been incarcerated.

Stephanie has been recognized for her service to the community and was the recipient of The One Nashville Humanitarian Award. She is proud to serve her community, one that reflects her family tradition and one that supports the well-being of her clients. Stephanie enjoys traveling and spending time with her husband, five adult children, and their seven grandchildren.

CHAPTER THIRTEEN
FROM DARKNESS TO LIGHT: A JOURNEY OF RESILIENCE AND TRIUMPH

CHANTA WILDER

DEDICATION

To my beloved son, Isaiah,

You are the light of my life, my constant inspiration, and the reason I strive for greatness. Your unwavering support and encouragement have fueled my journey, and I am endlessly proud of the incredible person you've become. May your path be filled with endless opportunities, and may you continue to achieve all your dreams. I love you beyond words.

To my family,

Though our journey was marked by struggles, I now understand the challenges you faced and the resilience that defines us. Your love and efforts shaped who we are today. May you find strength and courage to pursue your dreams, for it is never too late to reach for the stars. Let us continue to support each other, breaking the chains of the past and reaching new heights.

To my guiding light, my mentor, and my dad, Charles,

Your belief in me ignited a flame of determination. You showed me the power within, encouraging me to chase my dreams fearlessly. Your guidance has been my compass, and I am forever grateful for the impact you've had on my life.

To my loving husband, Kelvin,

Meeting you was a dream fulfilled, and the past ten years have been a journey of growth, love, and unwavering support. You've enhanced my life in every way, and I am grateful for the joy and stability you bring. Here's to many more years of shared dreams and beautiful moments.

With heartfelt gratitude, Shanika Chanta

FROM DARKNESS TO LIGHT: A JOURNEY OF RESILIENCE AND TRIUMPH
CHANTA WILDER

Disclaimer ** The story told below is the author's version of life events as they took place. The author recognizes that other people's memories of the events described in the book may differ from her own. The details are not intended to hurt, defame, or offend anyone.

My entire childhood was traumatic. I was in disbelief that this was the family I was supposed to have. I just knew I had been adopted and that there must have been a family out there that gave me away. I know God doesn't make mistakes, yet somehow, I did not belong here. There aren't any baby pictures to prove it, either. Even in my young elementary-aged mind, I knew I was different from the others around me.

Often, I would wonder what my life would be like if I lived in a different home, settling for my friend's home across the street from where we lived. I fantasized about what other families were doing at certain moments throughout the day. I wanted a family that played games, went to church together, had family reunions and summer vacations, and did things families would do. Instead, our family gatherings consisted of drugs, liquor, countless insults, and physical altercations. This was my normal.

As a child, I did not know anything else. Although my imagination would run wild thinking about the what-ifs and how I wish things were for my siblings and me, this was my reality, and there was nothing else I knew.

I grew up in a relatively large family in a home that was not quite big enough for all of us. It was almost as if there was a revolving door. Any of my grandmother's children could come back to live along with their children in tow, no matter the age or reason for their return. My grandmother and her husband always resided there, along with my mother and siblings, an aunt, and at least two uncles who rotated in and out periodically. Let's just say roughly eight people at all times resided in the home, along with three elementary and middle school-aged children, which were me and my two brothers.

Being the only young girl in a household dominated primarily by men was disheartening. With only one television in the home, it stayed on sports, and later in the evening, my granny would have it on the local news. Sometimes we had cable, and sometimes we did not. We were not the best when it came to financial literacy, so the cable would be on for only a short time. Mostly, we had bunny ears with aluminum foil balls at the tips.

I grew up with my two brothers, whom I love dearly. My older brother was a terrific older brother. There was nothing I wouldn't do for him. I loved him. He was smart, funny, athletic, and took care of me like a big brother would. At least he did when he was around. He was taken away on multiple occasions. At a young age, he got mixed up with the court system by hanging out with some guys who were older than him, and he just happened to be with them when they got pulled over by the police. I have more memories of my big brother being at group homes or living elsewhere than us growing together like we were supposed to. He was in and out of juvenile, and then that spilled over to him being in and out of adult jail.

We missed many of what should have been our formative years together. We remained close until our relationship turned sour when I was about twenty-one years old. I remember the exact moment when things changed. Keep in mind, he could ask me for anything, and I would do it, even when it included inciting me into illegal activities.

One day, he asked if he could borrow my car. I typically always said yes, and that day was no different. This time, I only had one caveat. I needed him to run by the bank to deposit some cash I had collected to pay my rent. I had planned to swing by the bank during my lunch break. Instead, I gave him hundreds of dollars to deposit for me.

The next day, I noticed the funds had not been credited to my bank. I called him to check to see what time he made the deposit, thinking it was possible that he missed the deadline, and it would hit the following day. After several excuses as to why the money was not there, it dawned on me that he had never made it to the bank. He continued to lie to my face for bizarre reasons as to what could have happened. After he gave me the runaround about the missing deposit slip, I gave up trying. I was hurt and would have never thought he, of all people, would disappoint me to my core. Not only was my brother letting me down, but now I could not make my rent payment on time.

After many years and countless times of him being in and out of jail after he stole my cash, I decided to forgive him. I wrote him a letter during one of his jail sentences and let him know that he would always be my brother and that I now forgave him. Although I was able to move forward with our relationship, things were never the same after that. I no longer allowed him to drive my car and the trust level was no longer there. I put myself and my safety first. I had to make tough decisions for my family, which often meant telling my big brother no.

I loathe talking about my childhood. Normal households are two parents raising their children, and my household was far from normal. I was raised by my mother and grandmother, who were both in the household. My grandmother was the head of the house. She made decisions for the family; however, they both greatly impacted how I was raised. My mother was a retired nurse and midwife. Although she took an early retirement because of her autoimmune disability, she had other hustles that kept her "working" and money coming.

She was an excellent cook and catered on the side. I attribute my love for cooking to her, as she cooked frequently for our large family. Due to her progressive condition, she often needed help opening jars, dicing vegetables, or taking large pans out of the oven because they were too heavy. I loved this time with her. From my first memories, until we moved away when I was in the 6th grade, it was my safe space.

When I returned back to live in my childhood home during my freshman year in high school, the relationship I once knew was not the same. My grandmother was gentle towards me but had a tongue sharper than a sword when it came to everyone else. It was amusing as a little girl when she was cursing her children out, but now the tables were turned. Although I do not remember her calling me out my name, she fussed at me and was so negative that if you tried to discuss anything remotely positive, she would have a rebuttal and tell you all the reasons why it would not work.

I only have recollection of my mom working a few times, and that may even be an exaggeration. I do remember going to work with her at a hotel. As a kid, going to work with your parents can be a great, long-lasting experience. I also remember this hotel because that is where she met a guy who supposedly swept her off her feet. I'm sure it was not hard to do, especially when you succumb to an environment of mental duress and oppression. He and my mom often shared the story of how they met. Whether they made it up or not, I will never know.

Allegedly, my mom was at the bus stop after work, and he was driving by and noticed her sitting on a bench. My mom is gorgeous, with beautiful dark skin, high cheekbones, and a slim face. It's not surprising that someone would be physically attracted to her. My younger brother and I liked him a little. Looking back, it was probably because things were just new. He would take us out to eat occasionally and then to a game room to have fun. We rarely got to eat out at a restaurant, so this was a great experience for my brother and me.

I rode the school bus to and from school every day, so I didn't have the slightest idea why he was waiting to pick me up from the bus stop at the end of our street. I mean, my mom was at the house, and it was a quick walk from the stop sign to our home in the cul-de-sac. Initially, I liked the fact that I didn't have to walk a few homes up alone, but I soon realized that this guy had ulterior motives. His white Hugo car would be right there waiting for me to hop in. This is when he started grooming me to touch his penis. It was only through his pants, which was probably a test at that point to see if I would tell anyone. I didn't say a word. Never. Not to anyone.

Shortly after dating, they decided they were going to move in together. We packed up our things and moved across town in the middle of my 6th grade school year. I can't remember if I liked this change, but I certainly liked the newness of living somewhere different and potentially meeting new friends. I was bullied from second grade up until we moved away, so I was sure there was some good that could come from the move.

I made some awesome friends that I stay connected with to this day. There was an English teacher in the 7th great who believed in me, and it showed. My basketball coach also encouraged me and was a positive light in my life. But other than that, it was mostly bad. Things turned bad when my mom got super drunk one evening. It's almost like he intentionally got her drunk. My brother and I shared a room at the time, so he called for me to go into the living room, which was steps away from where my mom and brother were sleeping. He had me sit on the arm of the couch and then pulled out his penis. I can remember the short, fat meat so vividly. It still makes me want to puke.

He asked me if I wanted him to stick it in, and I confidently said no. I thank God for the strength and knowledge to have the wherewithal to decline his advance. He then allowed me to go back into my room, where I could hardly sleep and now feared for my safety. Although he never tried anything like that again with me, it did make my life more uncomfortable. I didn't want to be there any longer, living under those conditions. A couple of weeks into my freshman year, I thought it best to go back to live with my grandmother. My aunt repeatedly asked me why I moved back into the family home. I never shared with anyone what I had endured. According to my aunt, the grass was not green enough to move back.

I still had questions, like who is my father? Better yet, who is my mom? Many years have gone by, and on top of the question of whether I belong in this family was, this may be the family, just a different mom. You see, my aunt and I favor so much with our fair complexion and light-colored eyes that growing up, many of my aunt's and uncle's childhood friends would mistake me for her daughter. After hearing that repeatedly throughout the years, I started to believe there could be some validity to it.

This aunt is smart, unafraid, no-nonsense, determined, and nurturing. I related to her more than anyone else in my family, including my mom. She left the family home as a teenager and never came back like some of her other siblings. We had that in common. I, too, left home at an early age and have been on my own since. I remember conversing with my aunt, asking her frankly if she was my mom, and sharing what I had heard everyone say. She was aware of those rumors, too. I have even heard her correct people who mentioned it. Yet, I still considered it in the back of my mind.

Now, I was probably only 14 at this time. Regardless of what I assumed, she ultimately denied the idea that she was my biological mom once and for all. At that moment, I believed her. I never second-guessed it for a moment after. She was convincing when she exclaimed, "No, NeeNee, BB is your momma!" I was relieved that I finally settled my uncertainty of not knowing who my mother was. I was then able to move on from questioning who my mother was to focusing more on who was my daddy.

I grew up hearing my grandmother share the story too many times of how I was going to grow up with a daddy. When I was nine months old, she carried me down to the numbers house and told my father that he had a child and he better take care of me. I am unsure how much time he spent with me as a baby and during my toddler years, but from my earliest memory, he has been there for me. We had a terrific relationship. He was loving and kind and provided security. He was gentle with me as a father should be to a daughter, but I have witnessed him be stern when talking to other men. He was there financially in my life. I would ask him for money for various school activities, and he would provide it.

As an adult, I would want money, and he would make me develop a plan to provide him with additional information on what to do when asking anyone for money. I would often have to discuss what the money was for, if I was going to pay it back and when, and what I would do to ensure I was getting financially on track.

We traveled together as a family, along with his siblings, my aunts and uncles. We went to the movie theater, and I even had an opportunity to spend the summer in his childhood town in North Carolina. These were moments I enjoyed spending with my biological father and his family.

Then there was this other guy that could have been my father. He was my oldest brother's biological father and has been around since day one, literally. He took care of my brother as much as he was allowed to. He was often met with opposition from my mom and grandmother. My grandmother would always describe him as a snake and say that he was always getting over on people. My brother even moved in with his dad at some point between living with us, another aunt, group homes, and juvenile. I had a jaded reality towards this guy because I was fed so much negativity about him.

I got a phone call from him when I was 14. I remember standing in the kitchen taking the call and not being able to travel too far because the old analog phone was mounted to the wall. I could hear the static from the faulty cord, and I had to twirl it in the perfect direction to make sure I could get clarity. I heard him say he wanted me to meet his daughter. I already knew of a daughter and a son that he had in addition to my big brother. This was another girl. He explained that we were the same age, and she was relocating from Knoxville to Nashville, and he wanted us to connect and hang out.

Alas! I would be able to escape this hell hole I have been smothered with for years. When she moved to town, we spent a lot of time together. I got to know her and learned more about how people my age lived outside of what I had been exposed to. Not only did I get to know her, but I also got to know her dad better. To this day, he is my dad, too, and no one can take that away from me.

During this time, we were able to cultivate a relationship, and I got to know him much better and see a different side from the rude and snide remarks my grandmother made about him. I began to realize that the majority of what she said about anyone was negative. It was rare that she depicted anything remotely positive and uplifting. I am grateful that I was able to learn differently about him. Not only did I gain a father, but I also attained much more than I ever had before. Someone who believed in me and helped me visualize what my life could look like.

I am pretty sure this is the time that I became rebellious. I had become conflicted from being in this whirlwind of chaos and a household that made it their purpose to either tear you down or hold you back and stop you from elevating. Now, with someone from the outside in my life providing a different and positive perspective, it confirmed that there was no way I could succumb to this environment any longer. So, I decided to run away.

I usually refer to this period as being homeless by choice. I could have stayed at my granny's house, where we were being chased by an uncle welding a pistol or finding butcher knives stashed around the house, including under mattresses and couch cushions. Even during the quiet times, I feared being in the home alone. Alone with a monster that lurked. I refuse to say who the actual monster was, but if I was impacted by this person, I wonder what my aunts and uncles endured during their childhood or early adulthood. I couldn't take it anymore. I would rather live in my car than be in this environment any longer.

For years, I lived out of my car and crashed from house to house of those that I met along the way. I spent my late teens and early adulthood in what seemed to be fight or flight mode, trying my best to get ahead and create a successful life, even if I didn't know what that meant. I knew I wanted more than what I saw in the world around me. At that time, the only way for that to happen was for me to get an education. Barely making it out of high school, I knew that getting a college degree was one thing I highly desired. I have yearned for only a few things, and walking across the stage was monumental.

There was always something in me that wanted to strive for greatness, even when I did not believe it. I have this internal ability and desire to want more out of life. I am always searching for the best circle of friends, ways to improve, and what I can do to ensure that my son will have experiences that I only dreamed about.

Although I have struggled through life for many years, I have encountered some great people on the way. Many have inspired and encouraged me through this journey. It would not be possible for me to be here sharing this story if it were not for my Tribe. My Tribe consists of those who have placed me in rooms I did not know existed, coached me on how to increase my knowledge, and never gave up on me when I was a hot mess.

Despite where I came from, I not only have an undergraduate degree but also a master's degree. Obtaining the graduate degree was the first time I was proud of myself. The first degree was great, but it was the minimum and something that I knew in my heart I would finish one day. However, walking across the stage the second time felt like I did something outstanding. For the first time in my life, I can honestly say that I am proud of myself. That little girl who endured so much is now a fully grown woman with so much love to share and knowledge to provide to others.

With my experiences, I want to build a platform for others to assist them in their journey. No matter what you are dealing with, what you have done, or what you are going through, there will always be light in a dark situation. I want to help people to see that. We are often so focused on what is going on around us right now that we are unable to see anything else. That is why it is important to seek mentors and also to read. Read everything you can about anything.

I received my undergraduate degree from Middle Tennessee State University. They did not have to accept me into their university. They believed in me, and by doing so, they helped me change the trajectory of my life over the many years that I spent at the institution. It has meant the world to me to give back to them and future students. I started an endowment scholarship to help those with the responsibilities of being a single parent and working while trying to obtain their undergraduate degree.

I am now in a place in my life where I know without a shadow of a doubt that there is nothing I cannot do if I put my mind to it. Not only that, but I have also grown to learn much more about myself and the power that I possess. I no longer beat other people's drums. I do things that I want to do, and if I do not want to do it, I don't. I surround myself with people who can enhance my life and avoid those who may take from it. My future is even brighter because I choose to be the light for others in their dark situations.

ABOUT THE AUTHOR – CHANTA WILDER

Chanta Wilder is a seasoned healthcare administration leader known for her dynamic blend of operational expertise. Holding a Master of Health Administration (MHA), she is currently associated with The Next Door Recovery (TNDR), where she brings years of valuable experience in orchestrating seamless operations and implementing meticulous compliance programs.

Throughout her illustrious career, Chanta has consistently made significant contributions to the healthcare sector. In her role at TNDR, she focuses on operations and compliance, striving for excellence and innovation. As an entrepreneur, philanthropist, and mentor, she brings a holistic approach to her leadership, driven by a commitment to healthcare advancement.

Chanta's dedication to continuous learning and expertise growth is evident in her affiliation with Lipscomb University, where she serves on the Executive Advisory Board. Holding a master's degree, she is deeply rooted in the academic community, contributing her insights and experience to shape the future of healthcare leaders.

Beyond her professional pursuits, Chanta actively engages in community service, contributing to organizations like the Junior League and YWCA. In Murfreesboro, she finds joy in family life with her husband, Kelvin, and son Isaiah. For Chanta, mentoring, community service, and travel are not just pastimes but sources of inspiration and growth.

Chanta's commitment to healthcare leadership is further underscored by her affiliations with the American College of Healthcare Executives and Leadership Health Care. This multifaceted blend of professional excellence, community involvement, and personal interests defines Chanta Wilder's holistic approach to life and work.